*After a beautiful day with constant winds from the
southwest, the mainmast is lit up by the setting sun.*

Jeanie Johnston

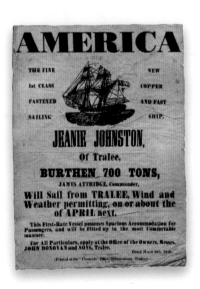

July and September 2005

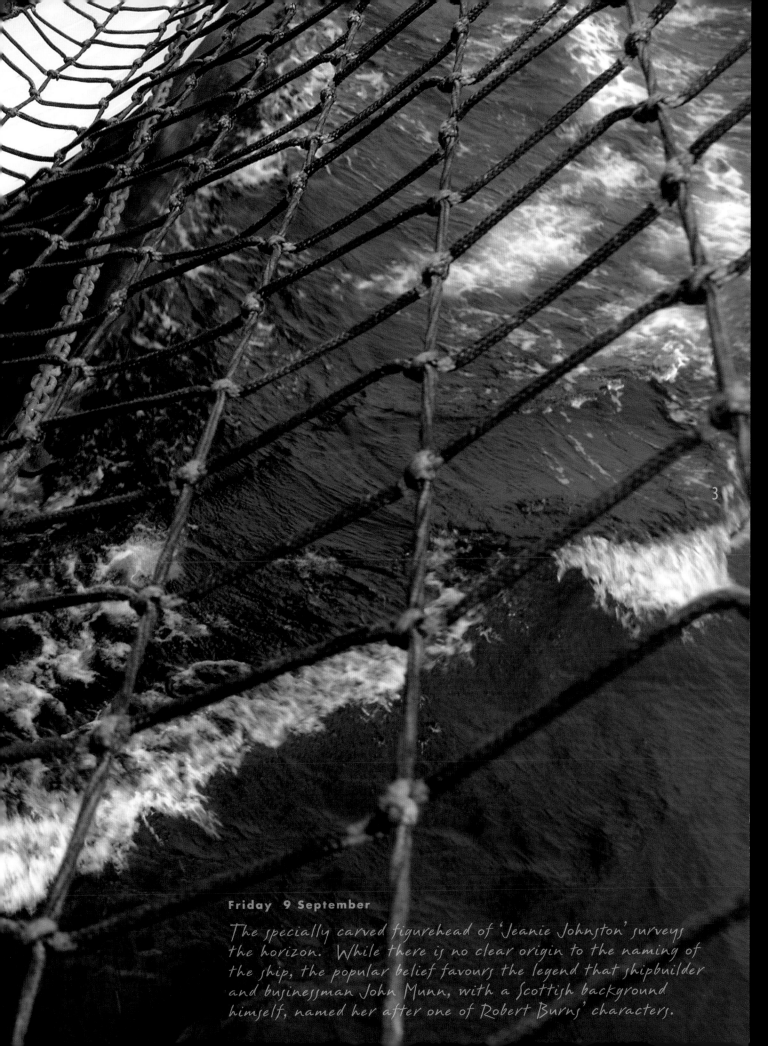

Friday 9 September

The specially carved figurehead of 'Jeanie Johnston' surveys the horizon. While there is no clear origin to the naming of the ship, the popular belief favours the legend that shipbuilder and businessman John Munn, with a Scottish background himself, named her after one of Robert Burns' characters.

3

For Tom, Daniel and Dairne

In memory of my mother, Rachel English (1923–2012)

This book is dedicated to those who initiated the Jeanie Johnston
project, to those who took part in the ship's construction
and those lucky enough to crew and sail her.

First published in 2012 by

The Collins Press,
West Link Park,
Doughcloyne,
Wilton,
Cork

British Library Cataloguing in Publication Data
English, Michael.
Jeanie Johnston : sailing the Irish famine tall ship.
1. Jeanie Johnston (Ship : Replica)–Pictorial works.
2. Seafaring life–Pictorial works. 3. Ireland–
Emigration and immigration–History–19th century.
I. Title
387.2'043–dc23
ISBN-13: 9781848891517

Design and typesetting by Black Mountain Design
Typeset in Myriad, New York, Eurazure and Futura
Printed in Poland by by Białostockie Zakłady Graficzne SA

All photographs by Michael English
Photographs taken during the ship's construction between 1999–2000
were kindly supplied by Peter Radclyffe – Shipwright.

Sailing the
Irish Famine Tall Ship

Jeanie
Johnston

Michael English

With special contributions by

Helen O'Carroll
Curator, Kerry County Museum, Tralee

Fred M. Walker
Naval Architect to the National Maritime Museum,
Greenwich, United Kingdom

Captain Michael Coleman
Former Master of the *Jeanie Johnston*

The
Collins
Press

The 'Jeanie Johnston' departs Waterford for Cherbourg in the 2005 Tall Ships race. Under very calm conditions, crew members release the course sail on the for'ard mast as she puts on a display for the waiting crowds with most sails set.

Friday 9 September

Having cast off an hour earlier the ship makes its way into Dublin Bay and the first bow watch of the voyage take up their positions on each side of the bowsprit.

Contents

Crew members start furling the topgallant sail on the ship's mainmast
as the wind drops. Under power and in the English Channel
the 'Jeanie Johnston' will soon have to cross the busy
shipping lanes off the north coast of France.

11

Monday 4 July

Maintenance of the vessel never stops as a crewman hangs from the 'horse', a foot rope on the course yardarm of the for'ard mast, and paints areas prone to corrosion, with Bray Head on Ireland's east coast in the background.

Heading for Dublin on a course of 348 degrees. With slackening southerly winds, the crew start furling the topgallant sail on the ship's mainmast.

15

'Sheets' for controlling the bowsprit jibs follow the graceful lines of the ship's timbers.

17

Wednesday 14 September

The ship heads west from Brest under power into the night. On her port side the light of La Parquette lighthouse bounces like a yo-yo in the swell that the ship is encountering. The navigation light on the mast illuminates the fo'c'sle in this two-minute exposure.

Tuesday 5 July

The ship's bosun cleans
down foot ropes accidently
painted with a tar compound.
Later in the day the correct
protective coating will be applied.

A lone crew member keeps watch for oncoming vessels in a heavy swell, off the north coast of France.

22

Two women gather potatoes as the sun sets. The potato was the staple food source for the native Irish and the crop's repeated failure over successive years due to blight led to the catastrophe that followed.

Historical Background

by Helen O'Carroll

Curator, Kerry County Museum,
Tralee, Ireland

Escape to a new life

Graceful and sleek, the *Jeanie Johnston* is a thing of beauty, and a testament to the skill, dedication and craftsmanship that went into building her. We are entranced by the possibility she trails before us – a life on the ocean wave that moves to the natural rhythm of wind and tide. Our senses quicken as we imagine our hands touching canvas, wood and rope, the crack and snap of sails in our ears, the tang of salt on our tongues and the briny smell of the sea in our nostrils, our horizons unconfined by office walls and city streets.

For us, a tall ship like the *Jeanie Johnston* is about escape: the dream of casting off the shackles of our ordinary lives and stepping into a simpler world where we can get in touch with ourselves again. We are as far as we can be from the elemental need for survival that drove our ancestors to sea in ships like the original *Jeanie Johnston*. They too saw the ship as an escape route, but they were escaping starvation, fleeing from a country devastated by famine.

The Famine began when a fungal disease struck the potato crop in 1845. It was an ecological disaster that had far-reaching consequences for a population over-dependent

on just one source of food. Crop failures were not new, but never before had the crop failed repeatedly, and it resulted in a social cataclysm that was to be felt for many generations both at home and abroad. In just ten years over 1 million people died and over 2 million left the country.

In 1847, such were the numbers leaving that people were packed onto overcrowded ships, some of which were unseaworthy. Many of the emigrants were already infected with contagious diseases and weakened by hunger even before they left shore. The worst affected were those sailing on ships to Québec: this was the cheapest route to North America and carried the poorest and most debilitated of the emigrants. Over 5,000 people perished at sea and 5,424 were buried on Grosse-Île, the quarantine station in the St Lawrence River. Thousands more, who had survived Grosse-Île, died in fever hospitals in Québec City, Montreal, Kingston and Toronto. The same situation was repeated up and down the east coasts of Canada and the United States, although not on the same scale. Almost 50,000 people died, a death toll so great that the ships that brought them across the Atlantic became known as 'coffin ships'.

'Than this scalp, nothing could be more wretched. It was placed in a hole, surrounded by pools, and three sides of the scalp (shown in the Sketch) were dripping with water, which ran in small streams over the floor and out by the entrance. Yet, wretched as this hole is, the poor inhabitants said they would be thankful and content if the landlord would leave them there, and the Almighty would spare their lives.'
Illustrated London News, *29 December 1849*

The term is often used as shorthand to describe the Irish emigrant experience in the nineteenth-century, even though the tragedy of 1847 did not recur. The 'coffin ship' experience was at the extreme end of a broad spectrum of misery for Irish emigrants, and it was the exception rather than the rule. The vast majority of the emigrant ships were not 'coffin ships', but even so the journey across the Atlantic was a feat of endurance. This was the first mass movement of people from Europe to North America, and it took place at a time when sail had yet to give way to steam, and on cargo ships that doubled as emigrant vessels. The concept of specialised passenger shipping had yet to develop, and transporting emigrants was seen as an opportunity to keep the ship in profit on the outward leg until more valuable cargo could be loaded for the return.

**Tuesday
5 July**

Shrouds on the port side bulwark and securing point of the ropes used for controlling the sails of the foremast.

The emigrants were berthed below deck, in the steerage, four sharing a six-foot-square berth, in makeshift quarters that would be swept away as soon as they disembarked so that the cargo, usually timber, could be taken on board. They brought their own bedding and cooking utensils. They provided their own meals from food they had brought themselves to supplement the ship's ration, which was sufficient merely for basic survival. The open hatchways provided the only light and ventilation; when they were closed in bad weather, people sat in the dark, which was pungent with the smell of sweat and

29

Friday 16 September

The bosun is helped by a deck hand to take
in one of the three jibs for repair.

A family, with mounting disbelief, unearths their stock of potatoes only to discover it is infected with blight and completely inedible.

seasickness, as well as urine and excrement from the overflowing chamber pots. Huddled together for a voyage that lasted on average six weeks, there was plenty of time to contemplate the uncertain future that lay ahead and to gaze into the abyss of what they had left behind.

You don't have to go as far as the 'coffin ships' to find a journey that challenged to the limit the resilience of people worn down by years of hunger. This was the experience for hundreds of thousands of Irish emigrants in the 1840s and 1850s. In the flotilla of ships leaving Ireland the story of the *Jeanie Johnston* is just one among many, but in its unfolding we see the people behind the cold statistics, hear their voices and connect with them on an individual level.

What's in a name?

The *Jeanie Johnston* was built by John Munn, one of the most prolific shipbuilders in Québec. His career encompassed the golden age of shipbuilding in that city and by the 1850s Munn had one of the largest shipyards in Québec. Between 1811 and 1857 he built over 100 vessels, including 32 fully rigged ships, 45 barques and 16 brigs. The Jeanie Johnston was one of four barques that he built in 1847, and, at 408 tons, it was the smallest.

'The fearful system of wholesale ejectment, of which we daily hear, and which we daily behold, is a mockery of the eternal laws of God – a flagrant outrage on the principles of nature. Whole districts are cleared. Not a roof-tree is to be seen where the happy cottage of the labourer or the snug homestead of the farmer at no distant day cheered the landscape.'
Illustrated London News, *16 December 1848*

The name of the ship is something of a puzzle. There was no Jeanie Johnston – after whom the ship might have been named – in John Munn's background, so we have to look elsewhere for clues. Shipbuilders often followed a pattern in naming their ships, and Munn was no exception. For instance, there is a very distinct pattern to the names of the six vessels that Munn built between 1850 and 1851: *Martin Luther*, *John Calvin*, *Pilgrim*, *Progress*, *John Bunyan* and *Covenanter*. The pattern is not so easy to discern in the four ships that he built in 1847: *Jeanie Johnston*, *England*, *Cromwell* and *Blake*.

Perhaps a clue is to be found in Munn's Scottish background. He was born in Irvine, where the poet Robert Burns (1759 – 1796) also lived for a few years. Some of Munn's ships are named after characters in Burns' poems, for instance *Jeanie Deans*, *Douce Davie*, *Highland Mary*. Burns wrote of a number of Jeanies in his poems, but not, as far as we are aware, of a *Jeanie Johnston*. Perhaps Munn decided on an amalgam of characters in order to get the full alliterative effect on the name of his ship.

Nicholas Donovan of John Donovan and Sons of
Tralee, County Kerry, owners of one of the largest
hardware firms in the region and who bought
the 'Jeanie Johnston' in Liverpool after the ship's
maiden voyage from Canada in 1847.

Charity begins at home

The *Jeanie Johnston* was launched in Québec in June 1847 and sold towards the end of that year to the firm of John Donovan & Sons of Tralee, County Kerry. The registered owners were John Donovan, the head of the firm, and his eldest son, Nicholas. It cost them over £2,000, the equivalent of around €238,000 today, and it was a sound business proposition. By 1847 theirs was one of the largest hardware firms in Kerry, with an extensive timber yard, warehouses and stores in the Square in the centre of Tralee. They owned some smaller cargo vessels that plied between Britain and Ireland, but the *Jeanie* was their first Atlantic trader. Previously, they had always chartered ships to bring the timber in, but in 1847 the number of ships involved in the emigrant trade was so great that it drove up the cost of chartering. It was also clear by this stage that emigration, hitherto unpredictable, was set to continue for a number of years. Buying a ship of their own made sense: they could send emigrants on the outward journey – on which the ship would otherwise be empty – and then load the all-important cargo of timber for the return voyage.

The Donovans combined Victorian philanthropy with a keen business sense. The *Jeanie Johnston* had a remarkably good record for an emigrant ship of the time, her passengers never having had a serious outbreak of disease in the seven years that she sailed between Tralee and Québec. This was because the Donovans took the trouble to employ a reliable captain and, unusually, a doctor on many of the voyages. But it was also because the passengers came from a 30- to 40-mile radius of the town of Tralee and the Donovans were astute enough to realise that word would travel fast if their ship was a disease-ridden tub with a hard-driving captain. A clean, safe ship would ensure continued business. That there were limits to their philanthropy can be seen from Nicholas Donovan's involvement in an assisted passage scheme on the *Jeanie Johnston* in 1851.

'*Another Sketch follows, which shows that, amidst this world of wretchedness, all is not misery and guilt. Indeed, it is a part of our nature that the sufferings of some should be the occasion for the exercise of virtue in others. Miss Kennedy (about seven years old) is the daughter of Captain Kennedy, the Poor-law Inspector of the Kilrush Union. She is represented as engaged in her daily occupation of distributing clothing to the wretched children brought around her by their more wretched parents. In the front of the group I noticed one woman crouching like a monkey, and drawing around her the only rag she had left to conceal her nudity. The effect was heightened by the chilliness and dreariness of a November evening, and by the wet and mire in which the naked feet of the crowd were immersed.*'

Illustrated London News, *22 December 1849*

In January of that year, William Denny, agent for the large Denny estate in Tralee, proposed that under the Poor Law legislation he would pay the passage money for a number of inmates of the Tralee Workhouse. He would advance the money and the Board of Guardians would repay him at a later date. Nicholas Donovan, who owned 1,200 acres of land northwest of Tralee, was also in favour of the idea.

The matter caused some debate because Denny and Donovan both selected workhouse inmates who came from their own estates, arguing that they did not see why they should fund the emigration of tenants from the estates of others.

Compass Binnacle

Salvaged in the early 1930's from one of the Donovan boats, The Co-operator and donated by Joe and Mary Galvin, Knockmoyle, Tralee.

It had been kept at the Galvin home (the former Donovan family home) in The Square, Tralee by Joe's father, Michael Galvin, who was Secretary of the Tralee Merchants' Association.

The firm of John Donovan & Sons Ltd., the owners of the Jeanie Johnston, was established in 1795.

Compass binnacle taken from the 'Co-Operator', a ship owned and operated by John Donovan and Sons of Tralee. This now resides in the Captain's Great Cabin at the stern of the 'Jeanie'.

Nicholas Donovan bore the brunt of the controversy: it was alleged that one of his tenants was not deserving of charity because he had been registered as a workhouse inmate solely for the purpose of emigrating; and that Donovan was taking advantage by sending his own tenants on his own ship and getting paid for it by the Board of Guardians. Donovan vigorously defended himself, pointing out that the man in question, James Stack, had lost a large farm during the Famine, and he was now living with his eleven children in a hovel made of wattles built against a ditch. He and his family would end up in the workhouse sooner rather than later and so it was better for all concerned if the money were provided for the family to emigrate. His argument proved persuasive and the Stack family left on the *Jeanie Johnston* that spring. Interestingly, the records show that when the ship arrived in Québec the Denny

'*On coming to Spanish Point, I found an enormous building, once called the Atlantic Hotel, converted in to an auxiliary union workhouse. It is an emblem of what is everywhere going on – the change from productive industry, to destructive pauperism, the cessation of hope and enterprise, and the spreading of apathy and despair...*

I send you herewith a Sketch of Driving for Rent. It may serve to vary a little the miseries I have to portray.'

Illustrated London News, *29 December 1849*

35

tenants were provided with £1 per family as landing money to get them started, while the Donovan tenants got nothing. Perhaps Nicholas Donovan felt that free passage on the ship was as far as his charity could stretch.

Captain Courageous

During the years that she sailed out of Tralee (1848–1855) the *Jeanie Johnston* followed a regular pattern, both in the times that she sailed and in her destination. Every April she left Tralee carrying passengers to Québec; the passengers disembarked and a cargo of timber was taken on. The ship arrived back in Tralee in late July, ready to exchange the timber for passengers, and left again at the end of August, arriving in Québec usually in early October. She generally left Québec in early November with a cargo of timber, on the way making a detour to Liverpool or Cardiff to discharge or take on crewmen, returning back to Tralee in March. The only deviation from this pattern was in March 1849 when the ship sailed to Baltimore in Maryland.

One of the remarkable things about the ship is the number of letters that the passengers wrote on arrival in Québec as testimonials to her captain, James Attridge, and which were published in the *Québec Morning Chronicle*. Testimonials to captains in this newpaper were not uncommon, but six to the one captain in the space of four years was unusual. Because some of the letters were reprinted in the local Kerry newspapers they can be seen as advertising to the home audience the merits of sailing on the *Jeanie Johnston*.

Mats from the 'heads'
are brought up on deck
to be scrubbed clean
during 'happy hour'.

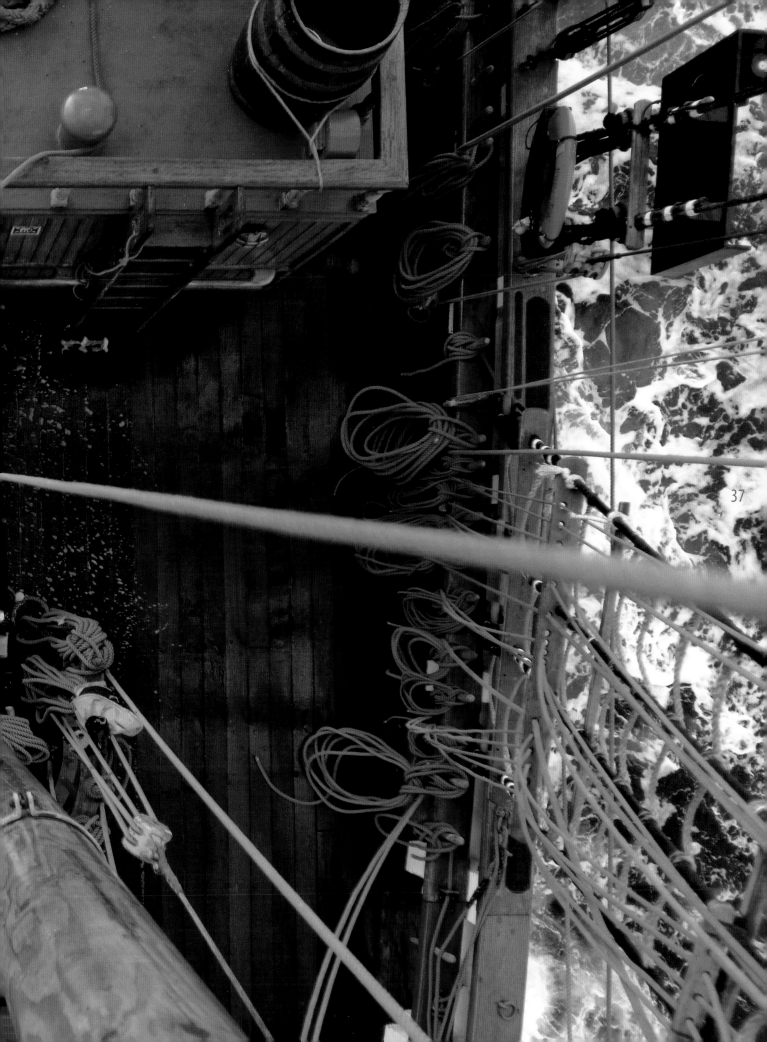

38

**Wednesday
6 July**

*'Jeanie Johnston'
takes her place
with other ships
in Waterford for
the Tall Ships
race to Cherbourg,
which will start
the following day.*

Furthermore, they were also an effective way of announcing the safe arrival of the ship and passengers.

But first and foremost they were letters of praise for the captain, and James Attridge was certainly a worthy recipient. By 1848, when he joined the *Jeanie Johnston*, he had been at sea for twenty eight years, twenty of them as a captain. He was from Castletownsend in County Cork and first went to sea as a fifteen-year-old in 1820. A ship's captain at the age of twenty three, he served on a number of ships before taking on the *Abeona*, sailing out of Cork, in 1838. He was master of the *Abeona* for ten years, making frequent trips to Tralee with cargo for the Donovans.

James Attridge ran a well-ordered ship and allowed no spirits on board. We know this because almost all of the ship's crew lists and agreements survive. Because of these documents we know substantially more about the sailors on the *Jeanie Johnston* than

'A specimen of the in-door horrors of Scull may be seen in the annexed sketch of the hut of a poor man named Mullins, who lay dying in a corner upon a heap of straw, supplied by the Relief Committee, whilst his three wretched children crouched over a few embers of turf, as if to raise the last remaining spark of life. This poor man, it appears, had buried his wife some five days previously, and was, in all probability, on the eve of joining her, when he was found out by the untiring efforts of the Vicar, who, for a few short days, saved him from that which no kindness could ultimately avert. Our Artist assures us that the dimensions of the hut do not exceed ten feet square; adding that, to make the sketch, he was compelled to stand up to his ankles in the dirt and filth upon the floor.'
Illustrated London News, *20 February 1847*

we do about the passengers: very few of the passenger lists exist today. Even though sailors lived transitory lives, moving from ship to ship, at this point in the mid-nineteenth century they are relatively well documented.

Between 1845 and 1854 all seamen had to have a Register Ticket Number and the Register of Seamen's Tickets contains detailed information on each seaman. For instance, Thomas Campion, First Mate until 1853, was born at Whitby in 1815. He went to sea as an apprentice at the age of fourteen: he was 5 feet 9¾ inches tall, with brown hair, blue eyes and a fair complexion; and he had an anchor tattooed on his left hand.

There were usually seventeen crew members on board, including at least two apprentices. They came from all points on the globe, one of them even from as far away as Valparaiso in Chile. There were generally a few desertions at Québec

as the crew were expected to help with the loading of cargo and no shore leave was allowed until this was completed. Another reason for deserting at Québec was the fact that sailors were paid a higher wage on the journey from Québec. For example, in June 1854 Morgan King, an eighteen-year-old from Tralee, was paid £8 (approximately €6,000 today) for the trip from Québec to Tralee, in comparison with the average wage of £3 10s (about €2,700 today) paid to sailors of equal rank who had signed on at Tralee for the round trip.

39

A forlorn woman who had failed to pay rent stands in front of her ruined cottage as the crowd who carried out the task make their way back down the mountain.

A life less ordinary

The *Jeanie Johnston* differed from many other ships in that a doctor was employed on board, and not just the usual ship's quack but a well-educated local man, Richard Blennerhassett. Most nineteenth-century ships' doctors had a terrible reputation. Many of them were badly educated at dubious medical schools and quite often not educated at all. Others were qualified but had failed in their careers, mainly because of alcoholism or incompetence or because scandal at home had necessitated a retreat to the high seas. The dilemma of trying to employ competent doctors who had qualified at recognised medical schools was one that defied solution until quite late in the nineteenth-century. The crux of the problem was that even if ship owners wanted to employ a doctor (which they usually did not), it was extremely difficult to find a reputable one who would put up with irregular employment, dreadful conditions on board, and a salary much lower than could be obtained on land.

In this context, Richard Blennerhassett was an exception. As a graduate of Edinburgh, then one of the most prestigious medical colleges in Britain and Ireland, and with a well-connected family, Blennerhassett would have had a range of more comfortable career options than that of a ship's doctor. Richard's father, also an Edinburgh graduate, was a well-respected doctor in Dublin and Kerry, and a regular contributor to the *Dublin Journal of Medical Science*. The large and extended family of the Blennerhassetts was one of the leading gentry families in Kerry, connected by marriage to most of the other gentry families in the county.

'*The Sketch of a Woman and Children represents Bridget O'Donnel. Her story is briefly this:- "...We were put out last November; we owed some rent. I was at this time lying in fever. They commenced knocking down the house, and had half of it knocked down when two neighbours, women, Kate How and Nell Spellesley, carried me out... I was carried into a cabin, and lay there for eight days, when I had the creature (the child) born dead. I lay for three weeks after that. The whole of my family got the fever, and one boy thirteen years old died with want and with hunger while we were lying sick."*'
Illustrated London News,
22 December 1849

Richard finished his medical studies in 1845 and he spent the next two years as the ship's doctor on board the *Bassora Merchant*, which sailed from Calcutta to Demerara in Guyana, transporting over 250 Indian labourers to the sugar plantations there. As an introduction to his new career, the journey on the *Bassora Merchant* was a baptism of fire, illustrating the reality of life as a doctor on the high seas. Almost inevitably, cholera, which was endemic in India, quickly made its appearance in the cramped steerage. Over fifty people died on the journey and Richard was obliged to despatch them, single-handedly, to a watery grave as the sailors were afraid of infection and the surviving Indians were afraid of defilement and loss of caste. There was very little he could do to minimise the scale of the epidemic as cholera thrived in the fetid atmosphere of the overcrowded steerage. Once cholera appeared there was very little that could be done to contain it beyond a wholesale purification, which was impossible while the ship was sailing.

Richard's odyssey on the *Bassora Merchant* affected him deeply, but did not dissuade him from a life at sea. Shortly after he returned to Ireland, he set off again, this time for Québec on board the *Jeanie Johnston* in April 1848. This was the first voyage of the *Jeanie Johnston* to Québec and Richard was to remain with the ship for the next four years. After the *Jeanie*, he served on two more emigrant ships, the *Lady Russell* and the *Ben Nevis*. In September 1854 he was employed as one of two doctors on board the *Ben Nevis*, which was scheduled to sail from Liverpool to Galveston, Texas, with 446 German emigrants. Soon after leaving Liverpool, however, a major outbreak of cholera on board forced the ship to put in at Cobh, and sadly, Richard died of the disease there. He was thirty-six years of age.

'*The ravages of disease at Skibbereen continue to be but too sadly confirmed. From a drawing made on the spot, we give a sketch of a scene of no unusual occurrence, as appears from the following extract of a letter from Skibbereen. "Deaths here are daily increasing. Dr. Donovan and I are just this moment after returning from the village of South Reen, where we had to bury a body ourselves that was eleven days dead; and where do you think? In a kitchen garden. We had to dig the ground, or rather the hole, ourselves; no one would come near us, the smell was so intolerable. We are half dead from the work lately imposed on us."*'

Illustrated London News, *30 January 1847*

All of the available evidence suggests that Richard Blennerhassett was far from being a typical nineteenth-century ship's doctor. That the *Jeanie*'s crew were of this view is clear from their parting gift to him of an inscribed surgical bone saw. It is most unlikely that they would have gone to such trouble had he been the average type of quack who served on board emigrant ships. After his death, his father, Dr Henry Blennerhassett, wrote a letter to the *Tralee Chronicle* outlining his son's career and including testimonials from Captain Smiley of the *Lady Russell* and from John Donovan & Sons. The Donovans wrote of Richard that, '*his reputation for skill and humanity were so great that one of the first questions asked before taking a berth by an emigrant was "does Richard Blennerhassett sail in the ship this voyage?"*'

43

Flight from home

For the *Jeanie Johnston*'s passengers the journey began at Blennerville, then the port of Tralee, but it was not a simple matter of stepping from the quayside onto the ship. By the mid-nineteenth century, a build-up of silt in Tralee Bay meant that large vessels like the *Jeanie* could only infrequently make it as far as Blennerville. Instead, ships came to anchor in the shelter of the two Samphire Islands at Fenit, seven miles from Tralee. Fenit Pier had yet to be built, so both emigrants and cargo were loaded and unloaded from lighter vessels sent down the bay from Blennerville.

This would have been the first time on the water for many of the *Jeanie*'s passengers, giving them a view of their native county from a new perspective just as they were leaving it for ever. The boat would be brought alongside the ship so that the emigrants could clamber aboard while all around them the sailors were busy getting the ship ready to sail, stowing luggage and shouting directions at each other.

The bone saw presented by the crew to Dr Richard Blennerhasset upon his leaving the ship in 1852.

A view of the bosun's store and workshop under the fo'c'sle of the vessel. While confined and cramped most running repairs needed on board are carried out here.

Bewildering and chaotic for people unused to ships and the sea, the embarkation process was just the first of many challenges in the journey across the Atlantic. It must have been an even bigger ordeal for a heavily pregnant woman like Margaret Ryal, scrambling up the side of the ship in April 1848. She barely made it on board before going into labour and the day before the ship was due to sail she gave birth to a baby boy. To mark the unusual circumstances of his birth the baby was named after the ship and her owner, and so Nicholas Johnston Ryal was added to the passenger list.

When they were planning their journey, Margaret and her husband, Daniel, must have known that the baby would be born along the way, but they decided to go ahead, even though the *Jeanie Johnston* was not the only ship they could have sailed on from Tralee that year. It is perhaps an indication of how desperate people were to leave. From every social class they surged out of the country in the late 1840s and early 1850s. This is reflected in the *Jeanie* passengers, from Daniel Harnett, who is listed as a 'Gentleman' on the voyage to Baltimore in 1849, to the very poor observed on the ship later that year by the emigration agent at Québec, A.C. Buchanan.

'The scene represented above is an attack upon a potato store in the town of Galway, on the 13th of the present month, when the distress had become too great for the poor squalid and unpitied inhabitants to endure their misery any longer, without some more substantial alleviation than prospects of coming harvest; and their resource in this case was to break open the potato stores and distribute their contents, without much discrimination, among the plunderers, and to attack the mills where oatmeal was known to be stored.'

Illustrated London News, *25 June 1842*

45

From her sixteen sailings across the Atlantic from Tralee, thirteen of the *Jeanie*'s crew lists survive. In comparison, only one full passenger list still exists, along with the fragments of two more. This gives us the names of just over 400 people, too small a figure to generalise from but enough to suggest that the circumstances of the passengers on the *Jeanie Johnston* were no different from those of the people on all the other ships leaving Ireland.

Whole families departed, such as John and Mary Ryle from Ballymcquin, who sailed to Québec in 1851 with their nine children, ranging in age from sixteen down to nine months. The composition of some of the family groups reflects the devastation wrought by the Famine, and Margaret Lynch, from Ballyheigue, was by no means the only young widow leaving with her children to find a new life on the other side of the Atlantic.

Some emigrants' passage was paid for by landlords, anxious to return their land to profitability by getting rid of tenants who could no longer pay their rent. In April 1853 65 tenants from the Earl of Kenmare's estate in Killarney set sail for Québec at his expense. The Earl had just inherited his title and, along with it, an estate burdened by rent arrears and defaulting middlemen. From his point of view, paying £220 (approximately €28,000 today) to get rid of 65 uneconomic tenants was the best way to finding a more profitable use for the land.

The *Tralee Chronicle*'s report was upbeat: 'A great many of those emigrated had very fair

1849						age	Occupation		Amt
March 10	Name	Residence	No	adult	Deport				
"	James Sullivan	Tralee	1	1 ✓		22	Sailor	£	4. 4 .
"	James Bailey	"	2	1 ✓		35	Mason		4. 4 .
"	Catherine Bailey	"	"	1 ✓		27	Wife		4. 4 .
"	Pat Bailey	"	"	1 ✓		4	Child		2. 2 .
"	John Bailey	"	"	" ✓		2mos	Infant		" . " .
"	Catherine Sullivan	"	3	1 ✓		21	Spinster		4. 4 .
"	Michael Cahillane	"	4	1 ✓		28	Labourer		4. 4 .
"	John Lynch	Brandon	5	1 ✓		34	Farmer		4. 4 .
"	Johanna Lynch	" "	"	1 ✓		32	Wife		4. 4 .
"	John Lynch	" "	"	1 ✓		6	Child		2. 2 .
"	Johanna do	" "	"	1 ✓		4	do		2. 2 .
"	Pat do	" "	"	1 ✓		2	do		2. 2 .
"	Danl. Lynch	" "	"	" ✓		Infant			" . " .
"	Pat Sullivan	Ardfert	6	1 ✓		40	Farmer		4. 4 .
"	Nell Sullivan	" "	"	1 ✓		38	Wife		4. 4 .
"	John Sullivan	" "	"	1 ✓		16	Boy		4. 4 .
"	Mary Sullivan	" "	"	1 ✓		14	Spinster		4. 4 .
"	Bridget do	" "	"	1 ✓		12	do Child		3. 5 .
"	James Sullivan	" "	"	1 ✓		10	Boy		3. 5 .
"	Jeremiah do	" "	"	1 ✓		8	Child		3. 5 .
"	Pat do	" "	"	1 ✓		6	do		3. 5 .
"	William do	" "	"	1 ✓		4	do		2. 4 .
"	Michael do	" "	"	" ✓		Infant			" . " .
"	Pat Fitzgerald	Tralee	7	1 ✓		24	Servant		4. 4 .
"	Johanna Sweeney	" "	8	1 ✓		20	Servant		4. 4 .
"	Bessy Griffin	" "	"	1 ✓		20	Servant		4. . .
"	William Hanifan	" "	9	1 ✓		21	Labourer		4. 4 .
"	Mary Rice	" "	10	1 ✓		18	Servant		4. 4 .
"	Thomas Rice	"	"	1 ✓		17	Servant		4. 4 .
"	John Reidy	Farmers Bridge	• 11	1 ✓		29	Smith		4. 4 .
"	Michael Dooling	Tralee	12	1 ✓		24	Cartwright		4. 4 .
"	Thomas Dooling	"	12	1 ✓		20	do do		4. 4 .
"	Julia Dooling	"	"	1 ✓		18	Spinster		4. 4 .
"	Edwd. Tangney	Mounthawk	13	1 ✓		23	Labourer		4. 4 .
"	Hanoria Creamer	Tralee	14	1 ✓		25	Spinster		4. 4 .
				32				£ 130 . .

Nominal List of Passengers p "Jeanie Johnston"

means of their own, but the passage money of the entire was paid by the noble Earl, while those in a less comfortable position were provided with abundant clothing and sea store.' However, the emigration agent in Québec, A.C. Buchanan, took a different view, reporting that 'there were a large number of very destitute persons on board the *Jeanie Johnston*, consisting chiefly of females and children who were coming out to relations in western Canada and the US, and they had to be assisted from the emigrant fund.'

The fare to Québec was £3.10s (approximately €2,700 today) and because it was the cheapest way to get to North America it was favoured by the poorest emigrants. The route to the United States was more tightly regulated and more expensive, and, as a result, farmers and skilled workers who could better afford the higher fare appear more often on the American passenger lists. For instance, in March 1849 the passengers on the *Jeanie*

'*A man of the name of Leahey died in the parish of Dromdaleague about a fortnight ago; his wife and two children remained in the house until the putrescent exhalations from the body drove them from their companionship with the dead; in a day or two after, some persons in passing the man's cabin, had their attention attracted by a loud snarling, and on entering, found the gnawed and mangled skeleton of Leahey contended for by hungry dogs.*'

Illustrated London News, *20 February 1847*

47

paid £4.4s to go to Baltimore, and a wider variety of skilled workers are recorded than on the Québec passenger lists, including a tailor, a mason, a blacksmith, a cartwright, a cabinetmaker, a shoemaker, a cooper and a dressmaker, as well as a number of carpenters and farmers.

Although it was the cheapest fare, £3.10s still represented a considerable sum for a labourer, almost half a year's wages in fact. Despite this obstacle, from the late 1840s and early 1850s the majority of Irish emigrants came from the ranks of the unskilled, poorest sections of Irish society. These were the surplus sons and daughters of small farmers and labourers, whose fares were subsidised by family members who had already emigrated. Chain migration quickly became a reality of Irish life and in 1850 it was estimated that £1 million had been sent back to Ireland from America to encourage further emigration.

Women left in almost equal numbers to men, a parity that was to remain a characteristic of Irish emigration right up to the present day. In this, Ireland differed from other European countries: elsewhere women were not encouraged to emigrate alone. In contrast, young single women contributed heavily to Irish emigration. Ellen Leyne, Julia Ferris and Bridget Brosnan, all from Tralee, Ellen Clifford from Obrennan, Bridget Houran from Chapeltown and Ellen Connor from Ballyheigue were just some of the eighteen-year-olds travelling on their own on the *Jeanie*.

There were a number of sibling groups on the Baltimore sailing in 1849, for instance eighteen-year-old Mary Rice from Tralee and her brother Thomas, seventeen; Julia Dooling

Detail of the 'top' or 'fighting top' on the mainmast which is sometimes incorrectly referred to as the crow's nest.

from Tralee, also eighteen, and her two brothers Michael and Thomas, both in their early twenties; Mary Donoghue, twenty and her brother Dan, twenty-five, from Killorglin. The sibling bond was a significant feature in Irish emigration, with brothers and sisters sending the money home to allow the next member of the family to leave, as well as looking out for each other during the journey and on arrival. The importance of this bond is even more poignantly illustrated by the youth of some of the siblings: fifteen-year-old Margaret Conway from Arda and her twelve-year-old brother John, travelling together to Québec in April 1851; or James Hare, sixteen, and his thirteen-year-old brother Denis, from Barrow, sailing to Québec in April 1854.

Ice, wind and snow

The journey to Québec generally took six weeks, four if the weather co-operated, but that happened only infrequently. Ice in the Gulf of St Lawrence was the hazard of the spring sailing, something the passengers would have been well aware of following the wreck in April 1849 of the *Exmouth*, which sank in forty minutes after hitting ice on the way to Québec. Over 70 of the 200 emigrants on board died, drowned or were crushed to death between icebergs. In April 1850 the *Jeanie* ran into large quantities of ice and in April 1854 she was trapped for six days before breaking free.

'I came to a sharp turn in the road, in view of that for which we sought, and of which I send you a sketch, namely, the packing and making ready of, I may say, an entire village – for there were not more than half-a-dozen houses on the spot, and all their former inmates were preparing to leave. Immediately that my Rev. friend was recognised, the people gathered about him in the most affectionate manner. He stood for awhile surrounded by the old and the young, the strong and the infirm, on bended knees, and he turned his moistened eyes towards heaven, and asked the blessing of the Almighty upon the wanderers during their long and weary journey.'
Illustrated London News, *10 May 1851*

49

Her longest journey was in the spring and summer of 1852, when it took her 74 days to reach Québec. She left Tralee on 14 April but two weeks later had to turn back because the ballast had shifted. Instead of the usual stone ballast, the ship had taken on iron in Cardiff in March of that year. In this period many ships carried an iron cargo as ballast to North America in order to meet the demand created by the expansion of the railways. It had a tendency to shift unless it was properly stowed, and shifting iron ballast was a common problem on emigrant ships in the early 1850s. Two weeks out from Tralee, the *Jeanie* had to turn

around and make for Queenstown (later Cobh) so that the iron could be re-stowed properly. It was 19 May before she was ready for sea again and it was the end of June before the 188 passengers reached Québec.

Gales were a feature of the autumn sailings and in September 1850 a three-day storm

Like the emigrants before them, the crew clusters on the for'ard deck to take in
the views as the ship makes its way up the River Suir to Waterford where it will
join the other competitors for the 2005 Tall Ships race.

52

A widely held assumption was that all emigrants were desperately poor. Here a more prosperous family seeking a better life wait to be called aboard while in the background a steamship heralds the dawn of a faster way to travel.

severely tested the *Jeanie*. Three years later, in October 1853, the ship was twice blown away from the Gulf of St Lawrence and eventually had to put into St Andrews, New Brunswick. Captain Attridge paid for 137 of the passengers to be sent on to their destination via Portland, Maine, but fifty-seven remained in St Andrews, induced by promises of work on the railway line. The reality turned out to be very different from what they had been promised. The work was irregular, the wages were poor and there was no fuel or bedding in the accommodation provided by the railway company. The passengers rightly concluded that under such conditions they would never be able to survive the winter and decided to leave.

'The accompanying is a sketch of a party of emigrants who have arrived on the quay after a long journey, in some cases close upon one hundred miles. They are stretched and tumbled about upon boxes and straw to seek some few moments' repose. This will show the extent to which the ruffianly touters and mancatchers carry their interference, and from which they are only obliged to desist upon the application of superior force.'
Illustrated London News, *10 May 1851*

The problem was that they had no means to travel any further. They decided that Thomas Jones, the emigration agent in St Andrews, was their best hope, and about thirty of them arrived at his house in the middle of a snowstorm. Jones provided for them for eight days while he tried to make contact with his superior in St John to see whether money could be found to to pay to send them onwards. He remonstrated with the railway contractors to no avail and had no luck either with his superior in St John. With no further assistance likely in St Andrews, most of the thirty decided to take the short ferry crossing across the border to the United States. They then proceeded on foot to Portland, Maine; for Kerry people bred in a milder climate that 250-mile journey through a freezing North American winter must have challenged them to the limit of their endurance.

Journey's end?

For most of the passengers Québec was not the end of the journey and many of them continued into the Great Lakes region on steamers that took them to the United States. The search for employment took them from place to place and contact between family and friends was often lost during the process of migration. The *Boston Pilot* newspaper had a column called 'Missing Friends' where people could place advertisements looking for each other. It was widely read by the Irish community and it had a national circulation of over 1 million in the nineteenth century.

The readership of the paper was not confined to Boston but covered the whole

northeastern area of the United States, and was read as far away as Louisiana and Florida. The poignant stories told in the brief advertisements bring home the reality of emigration in a way that few other sources can. For example, on 2 July 1853: 'Information is wanted of Denis Mahony, native of Beehenough, parish of Kilgobbin, sailed from Tralee three years last April in the ship *Jeanie Johnston*; when last heard from he worked in Pleasant Valley, Nicholas County, Kentucky. Any account of him will be thankfully received by his wife and two children. Direct to Ellen Mahony, care of Wm Garnett, corner of Genesee and Clinton St, Syracuse NY.'

Although the majority of the Irish arriving in America came from rural backgrounds, most of them settled in urban areas. Some of the *Jeanie* passengers bucked that trend, however, and continued working as farmers in the New World. Daniel and Margaret Ryal (also spelled Reilly), the parents of baby Nicholas Johnston, who had been born on board, travelled onwards to Liberty, Indiana, where Daniel got a job working on the railroad. Soon afterwards, however, they moved again, this time settling on their own farm in Silver Creek, Michigan. When he grew up, Nicholas left the farm and moved to Fergus Falls in Minnesota, where he worked as a bartender in O'Brien's Saloon. He married the owner's sister-in-law, and the two of them moved to Minneapolis, where Nicholas eventually opened his own wholesale/retail liquor store.

Another passenger who made a successful life on the land was Patrick Kearney, who was twenty-three when he sailed on the *Jeanie* to Baltimore in 1849. The following year he was living in Harford County, Maryland, working on the farm of David Ferris. Ten years later Patrick's position had improved: he was still living in Harford County, but by now he was married and had five children. In the 1860 census he was listed as a farmer, with his farm valued at $1,500, and his personal estate valued at $150 – the equivalent today of $31,500 and $3,150. His circumstances had improved to the extent that he was now employing a labourer.

55

'There are usually a large number of spectators to witness the final departure of the noble ship, with its large freight of human beings. It is then, if at any time, that the eyes of the emigrants begin to moisten with regret at the thought that they are looking for the last time at the old country – that country which, although, in all probability, associated principally with the remembrance of sorrow and suffering, of semi-starvation, and a constant battle for the merest crust necessary to support existence is, nevertheless, the country of their fathers, the country of their childhood and consecrated to their hearts by many a token.'

Illustrated London News, *6 July 1850*

Also on that Baltimore sailing was Daniel Dowd, about whom his descendant, John Kudlik from Pittsburgh, provided further information. Dowd had four children by his first wife, Julia Cahill; it is not clear what happened to Julia, but by 1849 Daniel had married again, and he and his second wife, Margaret, and their infant daughter, Mary, sailed on the *Jeanie Johnston* to Baltimore. The four sons from the earlier marriage appear to have followed at a later date.

Daniel acquired a 150-acre dairy farm in

Rough Weather *by Montague Dawson*

A three-masted barque similar to the 'Jeanie Johnston' pitches and rolls violently as it heads west through an Atlantic storm.

Rockville County, Maryland, and he also owned a row of buildings in Washington, D.C. According to John Kudlik, the milk from the dairy farm in Maryland was sent by canal to Washington, D.C. Daniel died in 1869. The farmhouse in Maryland is still standing, although it is no longer in the family's possession. Daniel's eldest son, John, (from whom John Kudlik is descended) worked on the railroad and eventually became a superintendent of a section of railway line in western Pennsylvania.

What is even more remarkable about the Kudliks is the fact that John Kudlik's wife, Susan Showalter, also has a connection with the *Jeanie Johnston* which came to light only when they visited Blennerville in 1999. She had spent some years tracing her family tree, and she knew that one of her grandparents was a Babbington from Currow, near Castleisland, County Kerry. What she did not realise, however, was that an

'…it may not now be out of place for me to send you a sketch of the interior of one of those vessels, which I accordingly do, and which I trust will readily explain the mode in which those vessels are fitted up, and where each party gets so many square inches to her or his share of ship, as the case may be, and where, if I am given rightly to understand, man, woman and child are obliged to huddle together like pigs at a fair. But then the ship is partitioned, divided, and formed exactly according to the strict letter of the law, and none can grumble, yet few can go on board one of them without being instantly struck with the chances that appear of the complete demoralization of the whole group.'

Illustrated London News, *6 July 1850*

59

earlier generation of Babbingtons from Castleisland had sailed on the *Jeanie Johnston*. In April 1854, John and Mary Babbington and their four children left Tralee on the *Jeanie*, bound for Québec. Their names were on a fragment of a passenger list that was discovered in Tralee at the end of 1998.

Loose gaskets reveal the wind direction across the surface of the topsail.

The sails are made from Duradon, a synthetic fibre woven from spun polyester with the appearance of flax or canvas. It also has the advantage of high UV and abrasion resistance.

To the bottom of the sea

By the end of 1855 the Donovans had decided to sell the *Jeanie Johnston*. Specialised passenger shipping, which had been slow to develop up to the 1840s, was now more common, and increasingly rigorous passenger legislation restricted the use of cargo vessels as passenger ships. The cargo/passenger trade was no longer as profitable and so the decision was taken to sell.

In 1855 the *Jeanie Johnston* was sold to William Johnson of North Shields in England. The ship became primarily a cargo vessel, trading between the north of England, the Mediterranean and Québec. In 1858 she was en route from Quebec to Hull with a cargo of timber, some of which was stowed on deck. The timber became waterlogged and began to weigh down the ship. As she sank lower the crew climbed up to the maintop, and after nine days they were rescued by a passing Dutch vessel, the *Sophie Elizabeth*.

Totally abandoned, the *Jeanie* was left to descend slowly to the bottom of the sea.

60

A young girl reads a letter to her parents who are illiterate and dependent on their daughter's education, gained following the establishment of the National Schools system in 1831.

A tale of two ships

The sinking of the *Jeanie Johnston* passed by unremarked except in Lloyd's List, where it was noted that she had been abandoned at sea. At the time, her disappearance was unexceptional because, for a basic workhorse of the sea, eleven years would have been considered a reasonable lifespan. Now, however, it seems extraordinary that it was functional cargo ships like the *Jeanie* that carried the first mass migration from Europe to North America.

The aim of the replica *Jeanie* was to recreate the experience of the nineteenth-century emigrants who sailed on these unheralded ships. The project also had many other ambitious and worthwhile aims, most of which it achieved: it created jobs; attracted tourists; boosted the local economy; provided skills training; passed on the traditional craft of timber shipbuilding; cemented already close Irish links with the USA and Canada; and contributed to the peace process through cross-border initiatives. By any measure these are all solid achievements.

What it did not achieve was to recreate the nineteenth-century emigrant experience: this is simply not possible. A replica built to modern sailing requirements and meeting twenty-first century health-and-safety standards can never replicate the experience on board a nineteenth century emigrant ship. In fact it gets in the way of our understanding of what it was like because it sanitises that experience. Equipped with a level of comfort unimaginable to the original passengers, it obscures the reality that, for them, there was no safety net.

There are two *Jeanie Johnston*s – the original nineteenth-century ship and the modern replica built in Blennerville, County Kerry in the late 1990s. Both ships are better served by remembering that each has her own story to tell. It is perhaps too soon for that of the replica because hers is a story that is still unfolding. And while it unfolds against a backdrop of economic crisis and recession, we can be thankful that it does not include the elemental need for survival that drove the story of the original *Jeanie Johnston*.

Monday 4 July

Gathering dusk slowly shrouds the ship as she heads
south into wind with just two jibs deployed. The last
rays of the sun silhouette Bray Head and the
Sugar Loaf mountain on the Wicklow coast.

65

Tuesday 5 July

There's nothing like the sea air to spark a strong appetite and crew members take full advantage of the fine weather and enjoy lunch on deck.

Sunday 11 September

The mainmast's port shrouds and ratlines, silhouetted against the course or mainsail on an unusually warm autumnal afternoon.

69

With the light fading fast and a change in the wind direction, crew members loosen the gaskets to let off the mainmast's topsail on an overcast evening in the English Channel.

Heading south in the Irish
Sea with a shower of rain
making itself evident on
the horizon.

71

Thursday 15 September

The view forward from the
helm of the ship. Choose from
the magnetic compass in the
binnacle or the digital one
located to the left of the doors
to the chart room. It takes
around twenty seconds for the
ship to react to a course change.

Primary Details

Ship Type: Three-masted Barque

Built: 2002 at Blennerville,
County Kerry, Ireland

Home port: Dublin, Ireland

Call Sign: EIJL

Weights & Dimensions

Displacement: 518,000 kg / 510 tons

Length Overall: 47m / 154 ft

Length on Deck: 37m / 123 ft

Beam: 7.9m / 26 ft

Draft: 4.6m / 15 ft

Rig Height: 28m / 92 ft

Total Sail Area: 645 sq.m / 6,943 sq.ft

Number of sails: 18 in Duradon

Length of rope used in rigging:
1,000m / 3,280 ft

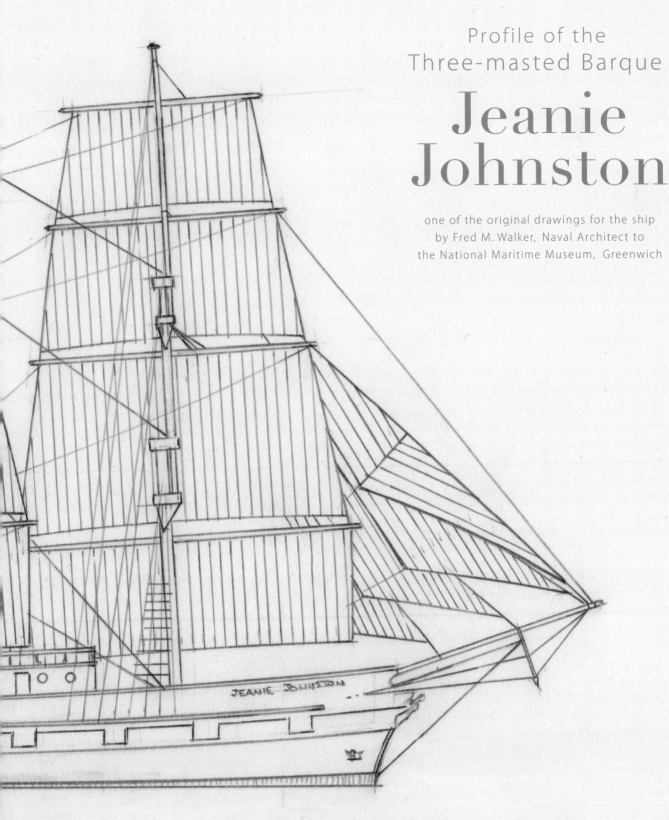

Profile of the
Three-masted Barque

Jeanie Johnston

one of the original drawings for the ship
by Fred M. Walker, Naval Architect to
the National Maritime Museum, Greenwich

JEANIE JOHNSTON

Materials

Hull Frames: Oak

Planking: Larch

Decks: Douglas Fir & Iroko

Masts & Spars: Douglas Fir

Safety Features, Propulsion & Electrical

4 Steel Bulkheads; 6 Watertight Doors
   and 5 Fire Doors

2 Caterpillar 3306 Diesel 280hp Engines

2 Caterpillar 3304 Generators producing
   105 KVA and 1 Emergency Generator

Crew & Range

Total: 40 with 11 Permanent Crew
   and 29 Sail Trainees

Range under sail: 70 days

Range under 1 engine: 17 days

Jeanie Johnston sails for America by Donal Stack

In this evocative painting, the 'Jeanie Johnston' starts her longest journey to date as she heads into the Atlantic bound for the United States and Canada on 18 February 2003.

Rebuilding the Legend

by Fred M. Walker

Naval Architect to the National Maritime Museum,
Greenwich, United Kingdom

The task of designing and recreating a historic sailing ship

Ireland has reason to be proud of the *Jeanie Johnston*. First, the replica project was conceived in Tralee, County Kerry and the designing, building, rigging, machinery supply and outfitting engaged a diverse group of people from Ireland and many other countries. The workforce at Tralee included nationals of Ireland, Australia, Canada, Denmark, England, The Netherlands, New Zealand, Scotland and the United States. In earlier years, shipbuilding in timber had small groups of nomadic shipwrights who worked around the coasts following shipbuilding orders, but in modern times these teams are much more international with workers coming from many overseas countries. The author (who has worked on similar tasks overseas) was delighted to meet many former colleagues in the shadow of Slieve Mish.

Secondly, while the overall size of the *Jeanie Johnston* (510 tons) makes her one of the smaller Tall Ships on the world stage, her appearance has been compared favourably with one of the most stunning windjammers afloat – the small but incredibly beautiful Danish full-rigged training ship *Georg Stage*.

The Jeanie Johnston of Tralee
Principal Builders and Designers.

This wooden panel, situated below the for'ard deck, records the names of those who took part in the construction of the ship.

Restorations

From the early years of the twentieth century, many well-known ships have been kept in good condition as a tribute to their past life or to some historic event in which they took part. Few of them are in full working order, but most are smart and in a condition which might be described as 'suspended animation', operating as museum ships, memorials or visitor attractions. Arguably the three best-known examples are HMS *Victory* (launched Chatham in 1765) and now permanently dry-docked at Portsmouth, the USS *Constitution* launched at Boston in 1797 and afloat in the same city in Massachusetts, and the superb Clyde-built tea clipper *Cutty Sark*, launched in 1869 and now dry-docked at Greenwich. Such restorations allow us to witness in a vicarious manner the seagoing way of life of former times and to marvel at the skill of their designers and builders.

Some restorations have been prompted by a realisation that a specific ship has unique connections, or perhaps is the very last of its type in existence: One such vessel is the recently restored British steam herring drifter *Lydia Eva*, which has the honour of being the sole survivor of the countless thousands of similar fishing ships built between 1900 and 1930. In this exceptional case the *Lydia Eva* has been restored to full working condition, a situation which under modern legislation makes it impossible for her to carry passengers, even on very short voyages; however, each year she makes the pilgrimage from Lowestoft to Great Yarmouth, re-enacting the drifter voyages of the East Anglian herring festivals of years gone by.

Courtesy of Peter Radclyffe - *Shipwright*

Close-up of one of the completed oak frames for the stern lying in the Blennerville yard awaiting installation.

Replica Ships

Interest in historic craft took an unexpected turn in the 1950s when the American naval architect W. A. (Bill) Baker, using well-researched historic information, produced plans for a replica of the *Mayflower* the ship which sailed with the Pilgrim Fathers to North America in 1620. This replica was built by an established shipbuilder in Devon and, with a volunteer crew, retraced the seventeenth-century Atlantic crossing in 1957. Baker displayed great enthusiasm for replicas; he felt they introduced a sharp edge into research and reacquainted modern seafarers – and also modern naval architects – with the ancient verities of their calling. More and more replicas were planned and built, with pride of place going to Captain Cook's barque *Endeavour,* launched in 1993 at Fremantle in Western Australia. This ship, described by many as the finest replica ever

79

Steeped in seafaring and boatbuilding tradition, Peter O'Regan participated in the construction of the ship as foreman engineer and later sailed with the vessel as its engineer.

built, has since retraced the three eighteenth-century circumnavigations of the man regarded by many as the greatest of seamen.

Other replicas are of a different type, like the *Vulcan*, a twenty-metre-long iron barge, which replicates the world's first iron ship, which was built near Glasgow in 1819. Another and similar replica is the wooden *Charlotte Dundas*, which pioneered steamship services on the canal system a few years earlier. Both these ships can be adjudged as educational exhibits rather than vessels for sea or inland waterway training.

In a period spanning about fifty years the replica ship has come of age and has become an integral and respected part of maritime heritage. Many of them can be found in the official Tall Ships Races in Western Europe and working on sail training and public relations ventures around the coasts of many countries.

The Irish Famine Ships

One of the world's great sea-borne migrations was from Europe to North America in the nineteenth and early twentieth centuries. By the 1840s, the small trickle of people making their way westwards was to become a mighty stream as the grim economic situation to be found throughout Europe worsened. The particularly difficult situation in the British Isles was even worse in Ireland where matters were exacerbated by an outbreak of potato blight coupled with several severe winters.

Emigration, despite all the entailed hardships, was for many years the only escape for starving, desperate people. Over the years hundreds of ships carried thousands of emigrants to the New World.

With the planning of a national commemoration of the 1845 Great Famine, thoughts turned to the building of a replica Famine Ship – a replica to represent the great fleet that sailed mostly from Ireland, but also from ports in England and Scotland to Canada and the United States. For reasons explained elsewhere in this book, the choice of ship fell on the *Jeanie Johnston*, a three-masted barque built in Québec in 1847.

Courtesy of Peter Radclyffe - Shipwright

Section of the ship's plans showing the numbered frames along with information on the deadwoods at the stern of the ship.

81

Objectives of the Project

The aims of the project were clear from the outset and it was proposed that the *Jeanie Johnston* should:

1   *Travel across the Atlantic to North America to commemorate those who made this journey in the nineteenth century, with a complement of at least fifty persons including the Master and a small permanent crew.*

82

In the ship's tiny galley the ship's cook Gerry Beggs starts the complex process of building a seascape using fish and other foods around a model of the ship for presentation to the crew later that evening at supper.

84

2	*The ship should be as close to the original as research, maritime legislation and practical considerations would allow.*

3	*The design of the accommodation to be such that a display of the Potato Famine and also the Great Migration could be set up when the ship was in port. This portable exhibition should enable guests to experience the ambience (both pleasant and unpleasant) of a crowded migrant ship in the days of dire poverty.*

4	*The ship to double up whenever possible as a sail training vessel, and hopefully represent Ireland in Tall Ships Events in Europe.*

Primary Objectives for the Naval Architect and Construction Team

It was vital that the following four priorities were applied in the design and building processes. These apply to all shipbuilding processes, whether the ship is commercial, military or as in this case a working replica:

1	*Safety of Life: the primary objective is to ensure that ships are designed and built with safety of life and limb foremost in mind for all working and associated with the vessel.*

2	*Safety of the Artefact: secondly, everything possible must be done to preserve the integrity and the fabric of the ship, as well as all cargo.*

3	*Sustainability: all materials of construction (especially timber) to be procured from sustainable sources and the ship, machinery and systems designed to avoid pollution. Recent legislative changes require that ships be designed for ease of recycling when their days of operation are over and breaking up commences.*

4	*Historic Accuracy: the ship to be built as similar to the original as historic research and practicality will allow.*

Timber Shipbuilding in the Nineteenth Century

By the mid nineteenth century, the shipbuilding industry was in the midst of the greatest change in its history. In 1819, iron ship construction was established and from then on the annual tonnage of iron ships built increased year on year, and by the end of the century, few shipyards were left building entirely in timber. This development was quite natural as, through the introduction of iron, the size of ships could stretch well beyond the length of 85 metres (an approximate figure), which was the natural length limit when building in wood. Furthermore, in the early years of the century and following the Napoleonic Wars, there was a scarcity of timber in Britain and Western Europe, a situation which was partially rectified when the great forests of Canada and the USA came on stream some years later. Then timber exports started to flow to Europe from the Maritime Provinces (New Brunswick, Nova Scotia, Prince Edward Island and Newfoundland – and also from Québec) and from the northeast States of the USA. This trade in timber was large in scale and took many forms, sometimes even the manufacture of special ships which were little more than well-constructed rafts of ship-shaped design which were broken up on arrival in Britain thus enabling timber to be imported with minimal duty paid. One or two Scottish shipyards arranged subsidiary yards in Québec, using their

Friday
16 September

Dolphins escort the ship up the Irish Sea as she heads back to Dublin having left Brest three days earlier.

skilled labour and taking advantages of the unique market conditions of that time. However, with a healthy demand for ships, the Canadians and the Americans capitalised on the situation and set up large numbers of shipyards dedicated to building fairly standard Atlantic sailing traders: Québec in particular had around thirty moderate-sized shipyards in the 1840s.

The typical North Atlantic Trader

The standard ship was the three-masted barque with a 'length on deck' of between 30 and 40 metres and a displacement fully laden of around 500 tonnes, indicating an ability to lift a cargo of just over 200 tonnes (known as 200 tonnes deadweight). Such ships could be built by an experienced team in well under a year, using timber (often fairly green and un-seasoned) from the Acadian forests. These ships had open holds, that is, no horizontal 'tween deck and no vertical bulkheads, making them nothing less than large open containers which were

Courtesy of Peter Radclyffe – Shipwright

The stern of the vessel with the oak frames secured to the keel. Part of the engine room now occupies this space while above it, the Captain's Great Cabin is located.

87

death traps in the event of collision or stranding on a rock ledge. The barque rig was three masts with the fore and mainmasts rigged with square sails and the mizzen (or after) mast with a fore and aft spanker sail. It was usual for the square sails to be four in number (occasionally three) and they were known from deck upwards as course, topsail, topgallant and royal; during the 1840s the topsail was a single sail, but as it became very large to handle was changed twenty years later and split as upper and lower topsails. Most had timber ports cut in the bows and often also in the stern, enabling timber cargoes to be loaded straight into the holds avoiding having to manoeuvre difficult loads through the very small hatches on the weather deck. The timber ports would be closed before sailing, carefully sealed and caulked tight for absolute watertight security on the ocean voyage.

Tuesday
5 July

The crew furl the topsail on the mainmast in preparation for berthing in Waterford.

Eastward cargoes on the North Atlantic usually were of timber heading for Britain and elsewhere. The westward voyage was different: on reaching an Irish or British port, the timber ports were opened and the timber discharged straight through the ship's bow and stern into barges or the quay. On completion of the cargo operations, sufficient timber would be retained to build a temporary deck in the hold, possibly 3 metres below the weather deck and on this a series of cubicles would be set up for the transit of passengers on the long leg to Grosse-Île, Québec or to New York. These cubicles would occupy a space of around 2 metres square by 1.5 metres high, each of which

Wednesday 25 August

A view of the bowsprit and the port cathead of the vessel, which many emigrants would have seen for the first time as they boarded the ship.

No. 8648 **Survey held at** Liverpool **Date** January 29th 1848 (Rec. 3/2/48)

on the Barque Jeanie Johnston **Master** James Attridge

Tonnage 384 / 408 **Built at** Quebec **When built** 1847

By whom built ______ **Owners** J & N Donovan

Port belonging to Tralee **Destined Voyage** Tralee

If Surveyed Afloat or in Dry Dock Dry Dock and afloat

Length aloft 106 Feet — Extreme Breadth 24 Feet — Depth of Hold 18 Feet 7/10 Inches

Scantlings of Timber.	Inches.		Inches Middle	Inches Ends
Room and Space	25			
Floors ... sided	13	Moulded	16	12
1st Foothooks	10 @ 11	"	—	10
2nd Ditto	10	"	—	9
3rd Ditto	10	"	—	6½
Top Timbers	9	"	—	6½
Deck Beams No. 22, Average Space 4 feet 6	10 @ 12	"	9½	—
Hold Beams No. 19, Average Space 4 feet 6	12 @ 13	"	12	—
Keel	13	"	15	—
Kelsons	15½	"	17	—

Rider ditto 14 by 10

Thickness of Plank. Outside.	Inches.	Inside.	Inches.
Keel to Bilge	3½	Limber Strakes	6
Bilge Planks	5	Bilge Planks	5½
Bilge to Wales	3½	Ceiling in Flat	3½
Wales	5	Ditto Bilge to Clamp	3½
Topsides	3	Hold Beam Clamps	4 & 7
Sheer Strakes	4	Deck Beam Ditto	6
Plank Sheers	4	Ceiling 'twixt Decks	3¼
Water-Ways	10½	Hold Beam Shelfs	5 by 16
Upper Deck	3¼	Deck Beam Ditto	—

Size of Bolts in Fastenings, distinguishing whether

Copper ~~or Iron~~.	Inches.	Copper ~~or Iron~~.	Inches.	Iron.	Inches.
Heel-Knee, and Dead Wood abaft	1⅛	Bolts thro' the Bilge and Limber Strakes	3/4	Hold Beam	1⅛
Scarphs of Keel ... No. 8	1	Butt End Bolts	3/4	Deck Beam	7/8 & 1
Floor Timber Bolts	1	Lower Pintle of the Rudder	3		
Kelson ditto	1⅛				
Transoms and throats of Hooks	1⅛				
Arms of Hooks	7/8				

(Written across: Size of the bolts not seen, but Reported to be as marked in the Column)

Timbering.—The Space between the Floor Timbers and Lower Foothooks in this Vessel is nearly close Inches. The Space between the Top-timbers is 2 @ 5 Inches. The Stem, Stern Post, are composed of Quebec oak the Transoms, Aprons, Knight Heads, Hawse Timbers, of Quebec oak and are ______ free from all defects.

The Floors and first Foothooks are composed of Quebec oak and Rock Elm. Elm in midship Timber, partly

The other Foothooks and Top Timbers of of Quebec oak & Hacmatack

The Shifts of the first and second Foothooks are not less than Not Seen N. B. *When less than prescribed by the Rule, state how many.*

The rest of the Shifts of the Frame are Not Seen

The Frame is well squared from the first Foothook Heads upwards, and ______ free from sap, and from thence downwards, the frame is well Squared

The alternate Frames are ______ bolted together. Not Seen N. B. *If not, state how bolted.*

The Butts of the Timbers are ______ close together; their thickness not less than ______ of the entire moulding at that place. Not Seen

The Frame is ______ chocked with ______ Butt at each end of the chock. Not Seen

The Main Kelson is composed of Quebec oak and the False Kelson of Quebec oak

The Scarphs of the Kelsons are not less than 6 feet 6 inches.

The Deck and Hold Beams are composed of Quebec oak Tamarac and Red pine

Planking Outside.—From the Keel to the first Foothook Heads the Plank is composed of Rock Elm

From the first Foothook Heads to the Light Water Mark of Rock Elm

From the Light Water Mark to the Wales of Quebec oak

The Wales and Black-strakes are of Quebec oak The Topsides of Quebec oak

The Sheer-strakes and Plank-sheers of Quebec oak The Water-ways of Quebec oak

The Decks of Yellow Pine State of good

The Shifts of the Planking are not less than 4 Feet 6 Inches. N. B. *If less than prescribed by the Rule, state whether general or partial, and if partial, in what part of the Ship.* The Planking is wrought 2 & 3 Strakes between

Planking Inside.—The Limber-strakes are composed of Quebec oak the Bilge Planks of Rock Elm

The Ceiling, Lower Hold, of Tamarac Between Decks of Red pine

Shelf Pieces of Quebec oak Clamps of Quebec oak

Fastenings.—To Hold Beams Double wood Knees, 2 Stringer 3 Pairs of Hanging Knees and 5 Pairs of Knees and Riders attached, the Riders [illegible] shown to take two bolts in the Substantial Part of the floors, the Iron Knees fastened with Iron in the Hold

Deck Beams Double wood Knees and Nine Pairs of Iron Hanging Knees and two Pairs of Steple Standards

Number of Breasthooks Five Pointers One Pair Crutches one

Butts End Bolts are of Copper in the Bottom, and One Bolt in each Butt End through and clenched.

Bilge and Limber Strakes Copper bolted through and clenched. Treenails of Tamarac

General Quality of Workmanship very good

We certify that the preceding is a correct description of the above-named Vessel,

Builder's Signature ______ *Surveyor's Signature* W Perkins

C. F. SEYFANG, PRINTER, FARRINGDON STREET, LONDON.

The Lloyd's
Certificate for
the original
ship which held
the crucial
information on
which the replica
was based.

would be chartered out to one family of four or five individuals. The return cargo manifest might show domestic goods and other items carried in the lower hold but, if not, the ship might well have poor stability and the crew would fill the lower hold with ballast made up of rock, shingle or sand.

The horror of travelling in these tiny compartments is beyond belief, especially when the holds might be battened down for days on end in violent weather, and the availability of hot food is zero. Apart from a small cubicle on the deck, usually for the use of ladies, there were no other sanitary arrangements.

As the years passed, emigrant rules demanded minimum standards of feeding, improved hygiene and increased deck space for each passenger. These rules promulgated independently by the British and the Americans would change the face of emigrant ships – and incidentally were in line with the rules for the carriage of fare-paying emigrants to Australia. Passenger accommodation did improve – albeit gradually. Almost all these ships were built without plans and none had their stability characteristics calculated in a scientific manner – only by the Master gauging the 'feel' of the ship from long and often bitter experience.

Courtesy of Peter Radclyffe – *Shipwright*

The stern of the ship showing the curves of the frames as they lead to the rudder prior to the planking being fixed. The rudder itself has yet to be attached.

The Corporate Objective

From the outset, it was clear that the *Jeanie Johnston* (built by Munn of Québec in 1847) was the preferred ship; she had been associated with Tralee for almost all of her life. With this in mind, the conjectural design was worked up. It was anticipated she would be a three-masted trader, barque rigged and probably just under 500 tons and would be constructed of North American softwood. There were no known drawings or paintings of the *Jeanie* as in those days such ships were built 'by eye' and with the help of some well-used and proven templates.

91

The Design Process

This was facilitated by a stroke of good fortune. The naval architect asked sundry repositories of ship plans and documentation to check if any papers were held for the *Jeanie Johnston*; no positive response was expected. Howerver, the Manuscript Department of the National Maritime Museum, Greenwich produced a Lloyd's Register Inspection Certificate dated January 1848 and signed in the Port of Liverpool, presumably on completion of her first transatlantic crossing. The *Jeanie Johnston* was given the very high rating 15A1, awarded in the nineteeth century only to ships of good construction and high-quality materials and with an expected working life span of fifteen years – quite a compliment to the builders in Canada! This invaluable document gives detailed information on construction and rigging as well as what until then had been elusive –

92

The mizzenmast, fashioned from a Douglas Fir, pierces the Captain's Great Cabin at the stern of the ship.

the hull dimensions. Even these certificates have their shortcomings and it is accepted there are inaccuracies possibly brought about by a surveyor working under the pressures of time, inclement weather and the inaccessibility of some of the structure of a wooden ship during a period of loading or repairing. However, this certificate enabled design work to begin.

Following the example set by the replica barque *Endeavour*, it was decided that the layout of the ship would encompass two areas; first the space below the 'tween deck, which is in line with the waterline, would be twenty-first century in all respects. Here the crew toilets and washrooms are sited, the machinery space is situated and a space incorporated for the vital fuel and freshwater tanks. This is to ensure that modern equipment is out of view when visitors walk through the 'tween deck to view the crew accommodation which after a 'make-over' each morning, is transformed into an exhibition site showing emigrant accommodation as in the days of the Famine. Incidentally, the passenger cubicles of 1847 vintage are designed to be comfortable crew berths while at sea and then in daytime converted to emigrant cubicles as part of the museum aspect of the ship. This clever switch-over was the result of a couple of positive conferences held with many of the Tralee shipbuilding staff during the ship construction.

Courtesy of Peter Radclyffe ~ Shipwright

The view aft from the bow as the first planks of larch are secured in place on the port side of the ship.

93

The weather deck is built as closely as possible to the times of 1847, and every piece of rigging checked to ensure it is in keeping with the times. Happily, several man-made fibres are similar in appearance to those of the nineteenth century and, even better to relate, modern and lightweight sailcloth is almost indistinguishable in appearance from the heavy coarse and difficult material that was in regular use 150 years ago.

Some Interesting Design Features

The settling of dimensions is of little importance here, but it is pleasing to report that on completion the ship is very close all round to the original. One small change had been planned, to increase the breadth by a small amount to improve stability and also enable better layouts inside for crews and for the museum displays.

However, on discovering that the old Tralee Canal was to be reopened, the original breadth was maintained in order to allow the ship (with a squeeze) to make its way to Tralee for winter lay-up. The canal locks were checked physically and the Engineer's Department in Dublin contacted, and all seemed to be going well until during the during the canal refurbishment it was discovered that the locks in the canal had 'battered'

*Crew members
await their
turn to make
the descent
from the upper
yards of the
ship's mainmast,
having furled
the royal and
topgallant sails.*

sides, that is the breadth at the base of the lock was less than at the top. The possibility of sailing up to Tralee was over for ever and the beam of the *Jeanie* remained steady.

Nowadays, all ships built under modern legislation must have keel-to-weather-deck bulkheads to break the ship into a series of watertight compartments. The Irish Department of the Marine insisted these be of steel, and once work commenced on this part of the design it became apparent that the ship would be immensely strong as well as having excellent subdivision. In the unlikely event of one compartment being holed on the waterline, special down-flooding valves are fitted to ensure all water drains to the compartment below, maintaining good stability.

The biggest change from the original ship to the replica is the fitting of two auxiliary diesel engines, three diesel alternators and a bow thruster unit to assist the ship when berthing in congested waters. The number of propellers was fixed at two, as a single propeller would either have to be off centre or the deadwood (the long skeg at the stern) would have to be cut with an inefficient aperture. Following this, a large (2.5-metre) scale model of the hull was tested at the Denny Ship Model Test Tank at Dumbarton. The outcome was a graph predicting the speed of the ship against machinery power outputs.

Now two key matters could be decided; first the size and power of the main engines, and secondly, from estimates of the longest voyages likely to be planned, the minimum amount of fuel required for 'safe get home'. This was assumed as half an Atlantic crossing under full power and required the fitting of fairly large fuel tanks. These were placed amidships in order that the trim of the ship did not change as the fuel was consumed.

Courtesy of Peter Radclyffe – *Shipwright*

A craftsman hammers home aluminium pins to secure the larch planking to the oak frames on the starboard side.

The selection of the main machinery was from a shortlist of three manufacturers, all well-known names with excellent reputations. After careful consideration the main engines were purchased through Irish agents from the Caterpillar Company. The ability to obtain spares on an almost worldwide basis and the large numbers of similar engines on the west coast of Ireland greatly influenced the final decision. The propulsors are two outward-turning five-fixed-blade propellers from a UK manufacturer.

The machinery exhausts are designed to leave the side of the ship, and here some ingenuity was required to ensure all exhausts maintained a suitable back pressure but also not admit water when the machinery was not operating and the ship was heeling under the wind.

As almost all machinery on the ship is electric, one of the most important calculations was the Electrical Balance, that is, the evaluation of maximum electrical power requirement for every operating situation, and from this the most efficient number and size of electrical alternators. While this sounds complicated, it is in reality a straightforward analysis, of which the following is an example:

**Thursday
15 September**

*All wrapped up
and on the helm,
steering 267
degrees.*

Ship under way with

1 *All pumps working*
2 *The windlass hauling up one anchor cable and the anchor clear of the bottom*
3 *All navigation lights on*
4 *The galley preparing a full meal for the crew*
5 *The bow thruster on stand-by*

On completion of the Balance, the worst-case situation is established and one can make a decision on the number and size of alternators. In this case two were chosen, again supplied by Caterpillar and installed alongside the main power units in the neat and compact machinery space. In addition, regulations demand a further emergency alternator which is positioned in a deckhouse.

International regulations now forbid the dumping of ship-generated waste at sea, except in special and closely monitored situations. As all ships accumulate sewage, the modern arrangement is that it is gathered in special holding tanks, and then treated in amazingly efficient treatment sewage systems before being dumped at sea as clean water. The United States Coastguard (USCG) is especially vigilant in this area, and indeed is surpassed only by the Canadian Authorities regarding the high levels expected of ships entering the Great Lakes. With the help of a British company, the *Jeanie Johnston* rose to this challenge and now sails with a state-of-the-art sewage disposal unit.

97

The Figurehead

The ordering of a figurehead for the ship was a matter of concern, as it quite unlikely that the original ship, built at minimal cost and bound for North Atlantic trading, had anything more than a decorated trail board at the bow. After discussion it was agreed to go ahead, as again this small item would distinguish the *Jeanie Johnston* while operating on the world stage. Now a feisty Jeanie with admirable cleavage adorns the bow of our good ship.

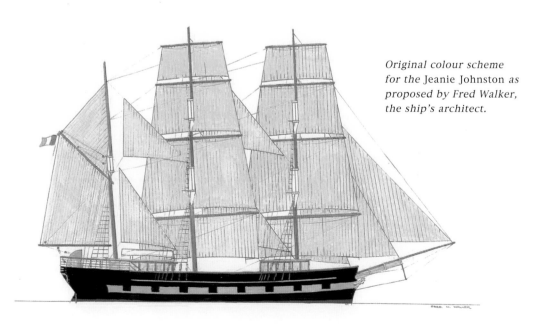

Original colour scheme for the Jeanie Johnston *as proposed by Fred Walker, the ship's architect.*

The Saga of the Postage Stamp

While nearing the end of the project the final hull colours for the barque were agreed. These were to be black topsides, green boot topping and deep golden-yellow painted ports – all selected to make the vessel stand out from the many other Tall Ships on the European scene. However one of the directors of the Jeanie Johnston Trust had astutely persuaded An Post (the Irish Post Office) to issue a commemorative stamp and agreed with them on colours of black topsides, red boot topping and white painted ports. Clearly An Post could not be seen to be issuing inaccurate illustrations and the colours of the *Jeanie* were accordingly altered to this livery. Hopefully, one day the more vibrant colours may prevail.

Launching

While it had been hoped that this, the most exciting moment in whole construction, might have been carried out in the traditional manner, the silting of the River Lee was to make this impossible. Rather than expend money on extensive dredging, it was agreed that the ship have a steel cradle placed under it and this in turn be lifted by a series of hydraulically powered bogies. The work was carried out by a ship movement firm from The Netherlands and the ship was lifted at low tide, without fuss and slowly wheeled down the building slip and on to a large flat-bed barge which was firmly aground. At high tide when the barge was afloat, it was taken down the river by small tugs to the Port of Fenit; there, the following day, the barge was subjected to a planned sinking and the *Jeanie Johnston* was afloat for the first time. That evening the ship was subjected to an inclining experiment, to check her stability – a test she passed with flying colours and all was set for the naming ceremony by the President of Ireland, Mary McAleese, on the following day.

99

Courtesy of Peter Radclyffe - Shipwright

Nearly complete, the Jeanie Johnston *awaits her first journey on the barge to Fenit where she will be launched.*

At the request of the President, the naming was without the traditional champagne, as Mrs McAleese was to remind us the ship was a wonderful way of commemorating times past but it also reminded us of the terrible years of suffering. An interdenominational Church service followed.

Final outfit

The final outfitting phase took place over the next year and while this ran relatively smoothly there was some bickering, as one might expect of an international workforce, uncertain of whether the ship would be completed due to the financial overruns that

**Friday
9 September**

Crew members make their way up the topgallant shrouds to loosen the gaskets of the mainmast's uppermost sail, the royal.

Friday
16 September

Having brought the royal sail down from its yard earlier, crew members fold it on the main deck.

hampered the project in its latter years. Happily these days are long past and the *Jeanie* is afloat and a reminder of the Irish maritime tradition, now a matter of national pride.

Some words of thanks

From the outset, all design matters were discussed with the Irish Department of the Marine, and all key plans and calculations were submitted for their scrutiny. Throughout the project, their assistance was friendly, steady and positive. The following internationally accepted 'rule-books' were used for guidance in the design:

Irish Merchant Shipping Rules and Regulations – Department of Transport, Dublin

Safety of Life at Sea Regulations (SOLAS) – International Maritime Organization, London

Rules for Building and Classing Wood Vessels – The American Bureau of Shipping 1942

Rules for Rigging Design – Germanischer Lloyd, Hamburg

One further volume was of inestimable assistance, namely Middendorf's magisterial work on sailing ship masts, spars and rigging:

Bemastung und Takelung der Schiffe – Middendorf F L Berlin 1903

In a project of this size it would be impossible to mention all who were involved – especially over a period that was longer than most expected at the beginning. However, one must acknowledge that the initial inspiration came from John Griffin of the Ashe Hall, Tralee and all the day-to-day operational requirements were handled by Michael O'Boyle, Ciarin O'Regan and his brother Peter, who later sailed as the Chief Engineer on the voyage across the Atlantic.

Many companies, both Irish and British, were generous with professional advice. One name stands out – Tommi Nielsen of T. Nielsen and Company. Tommi advised on the rigging and his company carried out the initial 'lofting' or full-size drawing out of the hull, a key part in the shipbuilding operation at their shipyard in Gloucester. The accuracy of their lofting and the skill of the shipwrights at Tralee enabled the sundry necessary hull dimensional checks before launching to be within 2 or 3 millimetres … that is excellent timber shipbuilding.

Bon Voyage, *Jeanie*!

101

Saturday 10 September

Under sail, in St George's Channel steering 183 degrees and making about four knots against a strong current. Under a lukewarm sun the ship heads for Brest in northern France with Land's End still some 115 nautical miles ahead.

Monday 4 July
The Captain takes
one last look around the
quarterdeck, having handed
over the watch to the first mate.

The mainmast's course sail 'clew' (lower corner) with the tacks and sheets for controlling the angle of the sail, starboard side.

With the wind slackening, crew members start the process of furling the topgallant sail on the foremast, seen through the sails on the mainmast.

Saturday 17 September

Looking aloft to the shrouds of the foremast. This is where you begin your climb on the ratlines. Tough enough in port but even harder when the ship is rolling and pitching at sea.

113

Thursday 15 September

*The ship's bow watch have been
recalled aft as the ship ploughs
into increasingly turbulent seas
and strong northerly winds
off Land's End.*

Captain's Log

by Captain Michael Coleman

Former Master of the *Jeanie Johnston*

The business of running a tall ship

The *Jeanie Johnston* is a three-masted wooden Tall Ship of some 500 tons, manned by a crew of eleven sailors, namely, Captain, First Mate, Second Mate, Engineer, Cook, Bosun, Bosun's Mate plus four Watch Leaders. When in sail-training mode we carry twenty-nine sail trainees, making up a total crew of forty. The Captain has to possess a Master's Foreign-Going Certificate of Competency. This entitles him or her to command any ship on any ocean worldwide and is an internationally recognised qualification. To command the *Jeanie Johnston* the Captain has to have relevant sailing experience and prior to taking over command of the *Jeanie Johnston* and I acquired mine on *Asgard II*.

The Captain has overall responsibility of running the *Jeanie Johnston* and is responsible for everything that happens on board and reports to the ship's owners. At sea the ship operates a watch system which allows the crew to effectively operate the ship 24 hours a day. The traditional watch system used is consistent and easy to remember so each crew member will have two 4-hour spells on-duty with eight hours off in between over a 24-hour period. Naming each as 'Foremast', 'Mainmast' and 'Mizzen' watches is common on Tall Ships and the Captain oversees the 08.00 to 12.00 day watch and the 20.00 to 24.00 night watch.

**Monday
4 July**

Crew members at work on the course yards of both masts, starboard side.

Thursday 15 September

Senior crew members take their supper on the quarterdeck instead
of below with other crew members as mealtimes will always clash
with the round-the-clock management of the ship.

The First Mate is the Captain's second-in-command and is responsible for organising the watches, maintaining the ship in good order, especially the sails and rigging. The First Mate is also responsible for training and safety on board and oversees the 12.00 to 16.00 day watch and the 12.00 to 04.00 night watch.

The Second Mate is in charge of navigation and communication on board together with documentation, paperwork and keeping the ship's logs. A major part of this is keeping the navigation charts and pilot books up to date and the Second Mate also oversees the 16.00 to 20.00 day watch and the 04.00 to 08.00 night watch.

The Engineer is in charge of the engine room and all things mechanical and electrical. The *Jeanie Johnston* has two main engines which are used to drive the ship when there is no wind. The ship also has two main generators plus a spare emergency generator to power all the electrical equipment on board.

The Cook is in charge of all catering on board and this is a big responsibility; remember 40 crew means 120 square meals per day, so the galley is a very busy place. Two sail trainees are appointed to help the Cook on a rotational basis. The *Jeanie Johnston* has an all electric galley which is much safer than a gas powered set-up.

Bosun **Boyce Nolan**

The Bosun is the Mate's assistant and is really the foreman on deck. Maintenance of the rig, sails and deck equipment plus the ship generally is his or her main priority and maintenance is an ongoing and never-ending business on a sailing ship with wear and tear always present.

The Watch Leaders are the deck hands and they organise and run the watches under the supervision of the Officers of the Watch. They also help the Bosun with the maintenance of the vessel.

Joining Day

This is the busiest day of a cruise and the day before the ship sets sail it has to be provisioned with food and other items for the trip ahead. Water and diesel tanks have to be filled, not to mention a good supply of seasickness tablets – yes, they are important for the first few days until everyone gets their sea legs. As the trainee crew members come on board they are allocated their bunks and sign on the 'Ships Articles'. Signing this document means they are legally part of the ship's crew and as such must obey all orders and commands. After a welcome-on-board talk from the Captain, it is straight into the joining instructions where the Captain lays down the basic ground rules to be

**Tuesday
5 July**

*Off the south
Irish coast with
Tramore abeam
and making
for Hook Head
under sail.*

followed when on board – mainly rules of common sense and safety. He then outlines the voyage ahead, the likely weather to be expected and the ports the ship is likely to visit. A voyage on a sailing ship is an adventure and is meant to be interesting, enjoyable, memorable and challenging.

After the Captain's talk it is the turn of the First Mate who outlines the basic duties and tasks of the trainees with a heavy emphasis on safety at all times. A lot of time is given to the correct procedures for climbing the rig, working on the yards, setting and furling sails in all weathers, day and night – this work is the essence and at the very heart of Tall Ship sailing. This presents challenges to most people and great satisfaction can be gained from meeting and overcoming these challenges. Safety harnesses are worn at all times when working aloft and on deck. When aloft the age-old rule of 'one hand for yourself and one for the ship' applies. To a landlubber, working aloft looks risky and dangerous but done properly and following the correct procedures it is quite safe. Coming face to face with fear and overcoming it makes for great character building. After the Mate's lecture there is usually a break for lunch.

*Watch Leader **Charlie Curran***

119

After lunch it is over to practical training on deck – the trainees are shown the ropes, as it were, then it is on to 'up and over'. This is their first climb up into the rigging, usually to the lower top, carried out under the close supervision of the Mate and Bosun. The first climb aloft is usually intimidating so it is best to get it over with early on – it is amazing how able crew become after a few climbs. Occasionally a crew member who is afraid of heights may baulk at the climb but usually before the voyage is over they will have overcome their nervousness. They are not compelled to do anything against their will – gentle encouragement usually works – and after a few days they are the first to spring into the rigging when ordered. After 'up and over' the crew practise the bracing of the yards, that is, swinging the yards from side to side, which is frequently done at sea to tack and wear the ship when under sail and to change course when the wind is against the ship.

The most important exercises of all are fire and boat drill. The accidents which are of most concern on board are fire, man overboard and a crew member falling from the rig and I will go over each individually.

The *Jeanie Johnston* is a highly flammable ship – she is constructed, after all, entirely out of timber and most surfaces are painted or varnished over. She is fitted with the

Captain Coleman surveys the radar and cross references sightings of vessels reported by the bow watch. While the radar is obligatory it cannot be relied upon to pick up everything, especially that of floating debris ahead which only the naked eye can.

Friday 9 September

The ship's bell is a gift from a corporate sponsor. Any major project such as this looks to both private and public sectors for crucial funding.

most modern and efficient of fire-fighting systems. We nevertheless carry out regular exercises simulating fires in various parts of the ship and going through the procedures to extinguish them, rigging hoses and deploying fire extinguishers and starting fire pumps. Of course, the most efficient action of all is prevention. To this end anyone caught smoking down below is put off the ship at the next port. No warning, no second chance: it is a very grave matter to put ship and crew at risk, so there is no appeal: it is off the ship and the Captain will divert the ship to the nearest port if necessary.

Watch Leader **Donagh Hennerby**

After the fire drill we carry out man-overboard and abandon-ship drills. All crew are assembled on deck and shown how to don the lifejackets and instructed on how to safely launch and get into a life raft. We carry enough life rafts for double the number of crew on board. Instructions and a practical demonstration are given on getting into a survival suit. The *Jeanie Johnston* is a very safe ship to sail on and our aim is to keep it so. To conclude the practical instructions we usually set and furl one of the topsails, going through all of the steps slowly and explaining everything clearly. This usually concludes the joining day.

Jeanie Johnston at Sea

At sea the life on board is on a 24-hour-a-day basis. The ship has to be steered; the lookouts posted and the sails set and trimmed constantly no matter what the weather, fair or foul, day and night. Meals have to be cooked and served and the tidy up done afterwards. Watches change every four hours and in bad weather it is a good feeling when one's relief arrives on deck at 04.00 on a cold and windy morning on a turbulent sea. However, mostly the weather is good and night watches have their own compensations. Sailing along in good weather on a clear and starry night is an unforgettable experience. The distractions of the land are left far behind and you become at one with nature and the elements – no TV or mobile phones or the pressures of modern living, just the ship, the wind and the sea and yourself.

At 06.00 the cook and the day workers are called. The watch changes at 08.00 after which breakfast is served, usually below, around the big mess table, but on deck if the weather is pleasant. In fact, one of the joys is having meals on deck when sailing along in fair weather with the sails aloft billowing into beautiful shapes and driving the ship along. After breakfast it is then into 'happy hour', which is in fact two hours, when the ship is cleaned from top to toe. The decks are hosed down and scrubbed, brass is polished,

123

galley and crew quarters cleaned and tidied and, of course, not forgetting the 'heads' i.e. the toilets. I should mention that everyone shares in these tasks except the Captain.

The watch changes again at 12.00 after which lunch is served, on deck if the weather allows. Usually the Captain will report on the voyage to date, bringing one of the navigation charts on deck to illustrate progress and the options available. This is eagerly sought after especially if participating in a Tall Ships Race, then it is back to the usual shipboard routine. One highlight of days at sea is encountering other ships, especially other sailing ships and trying to identify them. Occasionally we would exchange greetings on the VHF radio.

Watch Leader **Becky O'Laoire**

Sighting whales and dolphins is another memorable occurrence with the dolphins usually putting on a splendid display, swimming and playing around the ship at high speeds. Passing famous lighthouses and headlands are also highlights. The coast of Ireland is beautiful when viewed from the deck of a ship at sea. The Glens of Antrim, the Mountains of Mourne, and the Cork and Kerry coasts are particularly handsome from the sea. Sailing close to or between the Skelligs is an unforgettable experience, as is sailing off the Cliffs of Moher.

Usually on each voyage we practise a man-overboard drill. This consists of recovering a fender or something similar which has been deliberately thrown overboard. When under power we simply reverse the engines, stop the ship, launch the rescue boat from its position on the stern derrick and proceed immediately to the 'casualty'. When under sail it is not so easy as the ship has to 'heave to', that is, the main yards have to be braced opposite to the fore, or backed to the wind. This depowers the rig and stops the ship. The rescue dinghy is then deployed in the usual way and the 'casualty' is on board again in five minutes or so.

**Friday
9 September**

The view from the bowsprit as the ship heads south with all sails set to catch the wind from the northeast.

Occasionally if time and weather allow, we gather up everyone's cameras and place them with a crew member in the dinghy to take pictures of the *Jeanie Johnston* under sail. A photo taken in these circumstances is a wonderful souvenir to have.

The evening meal is at 18.00 after which the watch changes at 20.00 and then settling down for the night watches and grabbing a few hours' sleep. Sunsets are usually more beautiful at sea than on land. Picking out the various stars and planets is a favoured pastime of the night watches, along with identifying shore and navigational lights and lights of distant ships. Steering, navigation and observation are the main duties for crew

125

Thursday 7 July

A spectacular parade of sail as Tall Ships of all classes and sizes make their way down Waterford Estuary to Hook Head for the start of the Waterford to Cherbourg leg of the 2005 Tall Ships race.

Detail of the mainmast's course yardarm, port side with clewlines and downhauls running through single blocks.

to perform at night. Under sail the *Jeanie Johnston* usually makes 5 to 6 knots so usually we would make close to 150 miles each day. For long-distance planning we allow slightly over 100 miles per day – she is no greyhound, but she is not meant to be – she is a replica of an 1850 emigrant/cargo ship that was the workhorse of the ocean at that time.

Many of the photographs taken here were taken during the 2005 sailing season and the undoubted highlight of that year was the Tall Ships Festival and Race in Waterford, which took place during the first week of July. By any yardstick, the festival was a truly spectacular maritime celebration, probably the finest ever seen in Ireland. The huge turnout of the finest Tall Ships from over twenty-five different countries, crewed by 3,000 sailors, was indeed a magnificent sight to behold, a sight to quicken the pace of any sailor's heart. The forest of masts, spars and rigging lining both sides of the River Suir in the heart of the city was truly unforgettable. The logistical challenges this presented to the Waterford Harbourmaster, Captain Phillip Cowman, and his team was enormous, but all rose to the occasion magnificently. The sight of so many splendid vessels (over twenty Class A ships alone) gracing the quays of the historic Viking port will live long in the memories of the crowds of well over 300,000 who attended the festival.

The festival concluded with a dazzling fireworks display on the evening before the parade of sail which was special and historic. The parade was led by the three Irish square rig vessels; *Asgard II* captained by Colm Newport, followed by *Dunbrody* captained by Tom McCarthy and lastly the *Jeanie Johnston* captained by myself. It was a magic moment when the ships closed up off Duncannon Fort for a photo shoot. It was indeed a marvellous maritime experience, and to have been there leading the fleet was special indeed – one of life's golden moments.

129

*First Mate **Liam Kavanagh***

Many organisations were involved in the logistics of the event and they all did a wonderful job. Among them were the local pilots, the RNLI, the Coast Guard, the Air Corps which provided a fly-past, and the Army which contributed a 21-gun salute at the Reviewing Station at Dunmore East. Irish Lights provided the lights tender *Granuaile* as a start ship and, last but not least, the Navy provided the LE *Aoife* under the command of Lt Commander Martin Brett as a guard ship to accompany the race fleet to Cherbourg, France.

This was to be the very first occasion when a Tall Ships Race was to have been started from an Irish port. The fleet had previously visited Cork, Dublin and Belfast. However, this race start was not to be: to race we needed wind, and wind we did not have.

Thursday 7 July

The 'Jeanie Johnston', like many sailing ships of this period, was painted with what looked like 'gunports' in an attempt to convince and ward off attackers, such as pirates or enemy ships, from a distance.

It looked as if the ships had become bonded to Waterford. After five futile attempts to start the race, the race officers postponed the start until noon the next day and shifted the start line 60 miles to the southeast. The entire fleet motored over night; it was a surreal experience motoring on a mirror-like sea with the multicoloured ships' lights reflecting all around the horizon and with a full moon over head surveying the scene below. We got our start the next day but only just, the lightest of northwesterly breezes having set in. The breeze never really filled in and remained at a frustrating force, one or two at best. The *Jeanie* in very light conditions can hold her own: the big boys did not have the wind either and could not claw away from us. After twenty-four hours' racing we were placed fourth in our class and eighth overall, an incredible performance. A big cheer went up on board when I announced the positions on the tannoy. The race was called off the next day at 06.00 and the fleet advised to motor to Cherbourg. The final results put us well down the fleet; even so there were several notable names behind us. We were well pleased with our efforts; it is after all a fun event and participation is everything.

Second Mate **John Woodcock**

131

We arrived in Cherbourg on the morning of Bastille Day, 14 July – the French national holiday. Another three-day maritime extravaganza followed, marvellous hospitality as only the French know how, and boy do they love their Tall Ships, especially traditionally built timber vessels. The *Jeanie* was the focus of much attention and favourable comments and thousands visited the ship. The *Jeanie* did not continue on with the race series but sailed back to Cork instead. The Dublin Docklands Development Authority were in negotiations to purchase the ship and it was decided to keep her close to home. August was taken up with weekend visits to Dingle and Galway for Race Week. We also visited Schull, Cobh, Dublin and the return visit to Whitehaven, calling to the Isle of Man en route. The sailing season concluded with a ten-day return cruise from Dublin to Brest in France, all in all, a very successful and enjoyable season.

A lookout having spent the last half hour on duty is relieved with 'a fresh set of eyes' on the poop deck of the ship.

And to conclude I cannot do better than to quote that wonderful poem by that great sailor turned poet John Masefield it really evokes the magic of the sea and Tall Ship sailing.

Sea Fever

I must go down to the seas again, to the lonely sea and the sky,
And all I ask is a tall ship and a star to steer her by,
And the wheel's kick and the wind's song and the white sail's shaking,
And a grey mist on the sea's face, and a grey dawn breaking.

I must go down to the seas again, for the call of the running tide
Is a wild call and a clear call that may not be denied;
And all I ask is a windy day with the white clouds flying,
And the flung spray and the blown spume, and the sea-gulls crying.

I must go down to the seas again, to the vagrant gypsy life,
To the gull's way and the whale's way where the wind's like a whetted knife;
And all I ask is a merry yarn from a laughing fellow-rover
And quiet sleep and a sweet dream when the long trick's over.

John Masefield (1878 – 1967)   *English Poet Laureate, 1930 – 1967*

133

Wednesday 14 September

*As the 'Jeanie Johnston' meets increasingly heavy seas in the
Western Approaches, the bow watch crew continue to
monitor the seas ahead before being moved aft.*

Sunday 11 September

Two members of the ship's company
take in the overall scene below from
the topgallant's yard on the ship's
mainmast.

Wednesday 25 August

Looking through the ship's only skylight on the lower deck with the shrouds and yards of the mainmast in view.

143

Looking aloft to a full set of sails on both fore
and mainmasts with the staysail linking both.

145.

Reaching for the sky, the ship scales a large rolling wave in the heavy swell off the southeast Irish coast in early morning sunshine.

Thursday 15 September

Facing: Helmsman at the wheel. The quadrantal correctors are made of soft iron and are painted red and green, which signify port and starboard respectively. They, along with permanent magnets positioned underneath, counteract any magnetic interference with the ship's compass.

Detail of the ship's compass with a residue of salt lying on the surface.

OIL CHANGE M.E.P [2370]
OIL CHANGE M.E.S. [2390]
OIL CHANGE G.P. [7436]
OIL CHANGE G.S. [7207]
OIL CHANGE E.M.G. [16,214]
OIL CHANGE OUT.B. [4284]

MAINS STOPPED
O1115
SHAFT BRAKES
(ON)
CHANGED OIL FILTER
ON PORT GEN 7872

Coldharbour Marine Ltd.

Wednesday 14 September

Detail of the ship's wheel, showing wear and tear from time
at sea, a gift from the people of Québec.

Facing: In the for'ard area of the engine room the ship's
engineer cleans his hands of some oil before writing up on
the blackboard the most recent service work carried out.

Saturday 17 September

Sails on the mainmast take the full force of
strong winds from the northeast. The royal sail
at the very top remains furled as to have too
great a sail area set would put undue stress on
the mast and compromise the manoeuvrability
of the vessel in the current conditions.

Members of the current 16.00 to 20.00 watch crew, wait their turn for supper, which because of the balmy weather conditions is taken on deck, just off the Wicklow coast.

Saturday 10 September

Pitching heavily in the September gales the 'Jeanie Johnston' makes her way towards Land's End with the sun setting in the west.

Saturday 10 September

With no duties to perform crew members take time out for a break at the fo'c'sle of the ship in the late afternoon sunshine.

Facing: A large bulk carrier outbound from Milford Haven in Wales is observed on the port side as the ship heads south in St George's Channel. Constant vigilance is required by lookouts both fore and aft to ensure the ship remains clear of other vessels.

Friday 16 September

The Captain unfurls a replica of the first Irish naval jack with the Hibernian figurehead in gold.

Facing: Study of the bow, as the ship cuts through calm waters.

Friday 9 September

Two crew members enjoy lunch in a unique 'al fresco' setting.

162

'Happy hour' commences with cleaning above and below decks. With so many people living in such close proximity, general hygiene is taken very seriously, with a daily cleaning schedule designed to keep any viruses and bugs at bay.

Monday 12 September

Facing: Detail of the ship's lower mainmast which is made from a Douglas Fir. The cracks are a natural feature of the wood and pose no threat to its overall strength.

Having berthed in Brest an hour earlier a group of the ship's officers and crew gather on the quayside.

Sunday 11 September

Smoking is strictly forbidden throughout the ship but there is one place on the fo'c'sle where it's permitted. Fine when it is dry and sunny, dismal in lashing rain and high winds.

Facing: Looking aloft to the 'top' on the mainmast.

Crew members furl the topgallant sail on the foremast as the ship heads up the Irish Sea in the late afternoon sun.

Tuesday 5 July

The mighty four-masted Russian sailing barque 'Kruzenshtern' is sighted south of Hook Head, County Wexford.

172

Monday 12 September

Belaying pins securing various lines on the pin rail.

Facing: Having berthed in Brest, the First Mate along with a Watch Leader pull on one of the lines that will position the gangplank.

Tuesday 13 September

Facing: Departing Brest on an overcast and damp September evening, the 'Jeanie Johnston' is followed out of the harbour by an elegant French schooner.

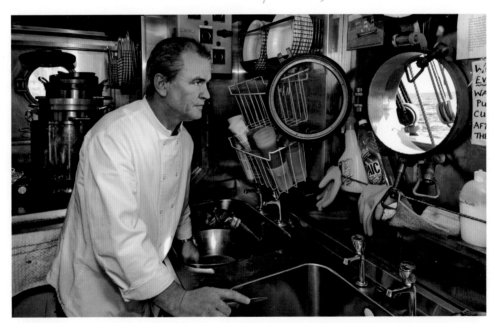

The ship's cook takes a break from preparing vegetables to view conditions outside the galley.

Detail of the foremast's course yard, port side, with both topsail and course sails catching the wind.

179

Saturday 10 September

A container ship passes astern in St George's Channel. Steel containers washed overboard from these ships pose a considerable threat to large wooden hulled vessels and yachts as some can remain floating just below the surface for weeks and will cause significant damage if hit.

Tuesday 5 July

The statue of the Infant Jesus of Prague has its very own berth.

Facing: The ship's bosun takes his position overlooking the fo'c'sle to supervise docking in Waterford. He holds a walkie-talkie to call out distances and communicate with the Captain and other ship's officers at the stern of the ship.

183

Thursday 15 September

Charlie Cullen shouts instructions to trainee crew members as they furl the topgallant sail on the foremast.

Facing: Detail of the clew of the course sail on the mainmast.

The Captain takes a dim view of the photographer who has made his way onto the quarterdeck as the ship enters Brest harbour. The quarterdeck is strictly off limits to the general crew when entering or departing port.

'Baggywrinkles' made from frayed
yarns are positioned on the foremast's
steel forestays to protect the course
sail from chafing.

187

Sunday 18 September

Facing: A permanent crew member sands down the wooden panelling outside the ship's galley prior to varnishing.

An early sun rise illuminates the Wicklow coast and the port side of the ship.

Monday 12 September

Fatigue takes its toll on a crewman as he dozes on the ropes of the gangplank in Brest.

Facing: The view astern from the mainmast's royal yard with a lone crewman at the helm.

On a bleak September morning as the crew take their breakfast below, the cook, his duty done for now, grabs a quick cup of coffee on the fo'c'sle with another member of the crew.

Friday 16 September
Captain Coleman indicates the ship's current position to the crew during a briefing on the main deck. Courses, weather, tides and other conditions affecting the voyage are outlined and discussed.

Sunday 11 September

Under way with a full set of sails on both foremast and mainmast, starboard side.

Facing: The ship makes progress against heavy swells while two crew members await instructions on the port bulwark.

Friday 9 September

Peter O'Regan replaces a bulb for one of the navigation lights on the foremast just above the course yard.

Facing: Daybreak outside the galley starboard side, looking towards the bow after a wet night.

A member of the permanent crew gives a coat of paint to the 'horse' footrope on the mainmast's course yardarm as the ship passes Dalkey, 7 nautical miles south of Dublin.

Thursday 15 September

'Jeanie Johnston' now under engine power, pitches and rolls in a gentle swell as she makes her way home just off the north coast of France on a sunny morning.

Aloft on the mainmast's topgallant yard with the sail partially furled as the ship heads northwards towards Dublin.

Detail of the masts and yards and
the intricate rigging of both the
fore and mainmasts of the ship.

Friday 16 September

Just some of the tools in the bosun's armoury for any running repairs the ship might need.

Facing: Morning light from the east illuminates crew members during a coffee break.

Saturday 17 September

Two of the ship's crew 'ham-up' a shipboard romance. While falling in love on a tall ship might be one of the most romantic of liaisons, breaking up on board ship certainly is not, so shipboard romances are neither welcomed or encouraged.

Facing: Bow watch crew members observe a passing container ship on the port side.

Tuesday 5 July

Dawn silhouettes the masts and yards as it approaches from the east. The single white light on the foremast indicates to other shipping that the ship is under engine power and not sail.

213

214

The small but businesslike chart room is situated on the quarterdeck of the vessel and is equipped with all the latest navigational and safety equipment required for today's maritime environment.

Friday 9 September

On watch at the bow with the three jibs ready to be deployed. The solid piece of timber in the foreground is the starboard cathead which juts out over the side of the ship and was used to lower and raise the anchors in earlier times. Two conventional anchors operated by electrical power are now used for mooring the vessel away from quays.

Wednesday 14 September

Facing: Crew members struggle to loosen gaskets and release the course sail on the mainmast on a dull morning.

View looking aft along the starboard side of the ship with just the staysails set.

Sunday 11 September

Permanent crew members prepare the surfaces of the electric windlass for a fresh coat of paint.

Facing: Study of spare blocks in the bosun's store.

223

Bleak beginning to a new
day south of Land's End,
but with the prospect of
better weather to come.

225

Heading north back to Dublin in the Irish Sea with Wales just over the horizon. In calm conditions and with no wind from the southwest forecast the crew furl the course sail on the ship's foremast.

Thursday 15 September

After a good night's sleep below deck, your first view of the current weather conditions is through one of the four doors to the main deck.

Facing: The ship's engineer removes spent oil canisters having topped up one of the ship's four diesel engines.

Saturday 17 September

The photographer gets himself into the frame.

Facing: Detail of topsail and topgallant yards with their
sails on the for'ard mast, port side.

Sunday 18 September

Members of the crew cluster on the topsail yard as they furl the sail in calm conditions.

Friday 9 September

Detail of starboard triple block and shackle.

Facing: The bosun makes his way back along the topsail yard having made some running repairs to the sail on the mainmast.

Saturday 17 September

Crew members furl both course and topsails on the ship's mainmast.

Facing: Sunset in St George's Channel illuminates the mainmast's 'top' with a full set of sails.

236

Under an overcast sky the 'Jeanie Johnston' takes her place in Waterford in a scene that could have been photographed over a hundred years ago. Only some recent building activity gives a clue to more modern times.

Friday 9 September

*A crew member descends
the futtock shroud, port
side of the mainmast in
St George's Channel.*

239

Thursday 15 September

'Jeanie Johnston' faces into a strong northerly wind, as she encounters a heavy swell off Land's End prior to meeting a rogue wave, some 6 metres high.

Thursday 15 September

Under a blanket of mist the ship heads north on the homeward leg of the voyage from Brest as dawn begins to break to starboard.

Friday 16 September

Crew furl the topgallant sail on the mainmast.

Facing: Everyone gets the chance to take the helm during both day and night watches and experience what it is like to steer a Tall Ship. Ironically it is easier to hold a steady course under sail than engine power.

Friday 9 September

Detail of the course yard, starboard side, with course and topsail set.

Facing: Crew members enjoy the early morning sun as they sit atop the topgallant yard on mainmast awaiting orders.

Friday 9 September

Members of the mainmast watch, or the 16.00 to 20.00 watch and named after the tallest mast of the ship, gather on the quarterdeck in the late afternoon awaiting new orders.

The view ahead showing the navigation
lights on the foremast which are specially
positioned and provide maximum visibility
for the ship at night in clear conditions.

251

252

Tuesday 13 September

Detail of secured bunt and clewlines on the pin rail.

Facing: The ship's bell gets special attention as it is made of brass which gets easily tarnished at sea by the salty spray.

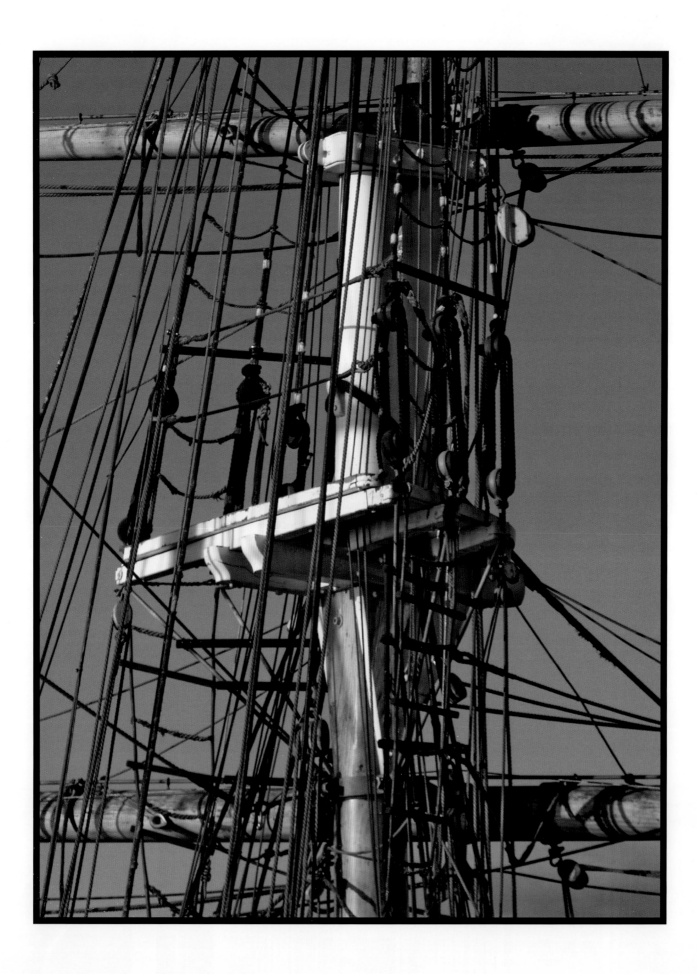

Saturday 17 September

Facing: Detail of the main 'top' and the links of the lower masthead and heel of the topmast on the ship's mainmast.

In mid December of 1858, en route from Québec to Hull with a cargo of timber the original 'Jeanie Johnston' became waterlogged and started to sink. It was on this precarious platform halfway up the masts that the crew of the original ship survived for nine days before being rescued by a Dutch ship, the 'Sophie Elizabeth'.

Crew members secure buntlines on the fife rail at the foot of the foremast.

COMMEMORATING THE
JEANIE JOHNSTON MILLENNIUM VOYAGE

The Members of the United States Coast Guard Auxiliary

"Salute the Vision"

of the Jeanie Johnston's Builders
and the courage and commitment of her Officers and Crew.
We wish you a safe and successful voyage
and extend a hearty welcome to American waters.

In the spirit of an old Irish Blessing

"May Your Winds Be Fresh.
Your Sails Full.
And Your Wake Clean And Straight."

Everette L. Tucker, Jr.
National Commodore

May 2000

**Sunday
18 September**

The exposed oak frames in the Captain's Great Cabin reveal the lines of the ship's hull at the stern of the vessel...

Certificates and crests that adorn the sides are from the ports that the ship has visited.

A crew member coils one of the
buntlines that was used to haul
in the topsail on the foremast
prior to furling.

261

Tuesday 5 July

As the ship nears Waterford, crew members furl the topgallant sail on the mainmast. In keeping with maritime tradition the crew furl the sails much tighter to the yard for port visits. The way a ship is presented in port reflects on the crew who sail her.

Stretching out on the netting of the ship's bowsprit. With just the the sea below you it is, without doubt, the most comfortable and relaxing place on the planet.

263

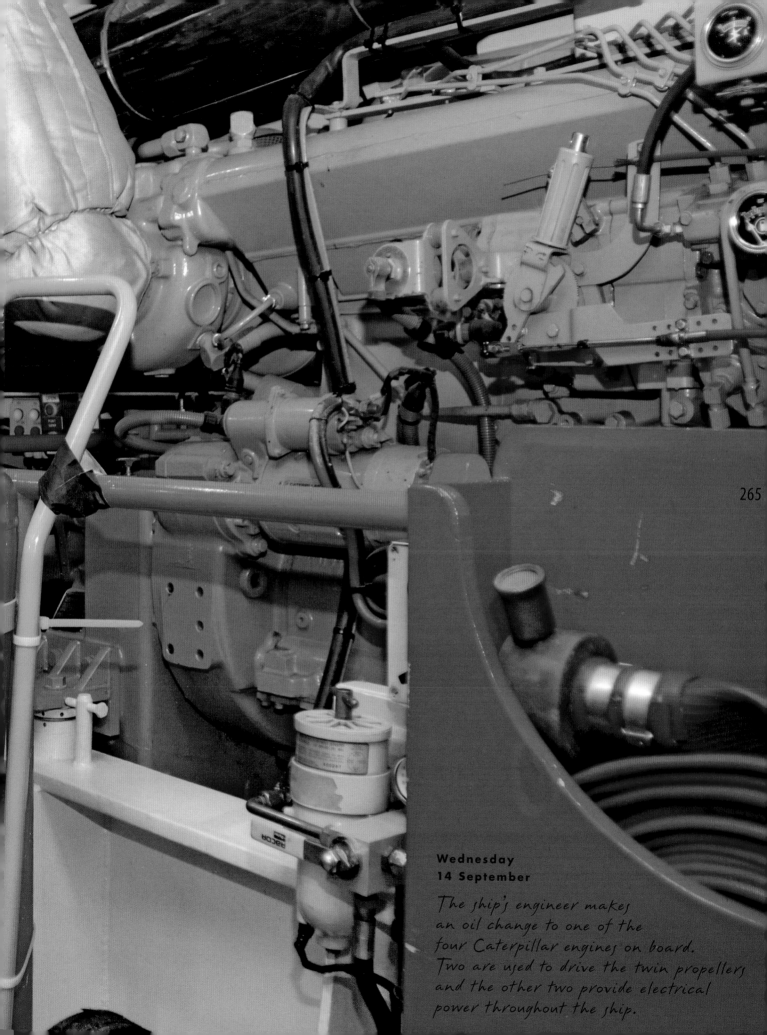

**Wednesday
14 September**

*The ship's engineer makes
an oil change to one of the
four Caterpillar engines on board.
Two are used to drive the twin propellers
and the other two provide electrical
power throughout the ship.*

Wednesday 25 August

*Looking aloft to the 'top' on
the mainmast with the
four yards, rigging
and shrouds.*

Tuesday 5 July

Journey's end... Under an overcast sky the 'Jeanie Johnston' edges her way upriver past the US Coast Guard Tall Ship 'Eagle' towards her berth in the centre of Waterford.

269

Thursday 7 July

Sailing into an uncertain future – 'Jeanie Johnston' follows the 'Dunbrody,' a similar replica famine ship, in Waterford Estuary. Both ships, having been built during the affluent Celtic Tiger years, will require considerable amounts of money for their continued upkeep amid one of Ireland's worst recessions.

Credits

'America' Poster 1
Courtesy of Kerry County Museum, Tralee

Potato Gatherers in the West 24
by Charles McIver Grierson
Courtesy of the Crawford Gallery, Cork

Irish Famine Illustrations 27–59
from the *Illustrated London News*
Courtesy of 'Views of the Famine' Website

Discovery of Potato Blight 30
by Daniel MacDonald
Courtesy of the Irish Folklore Collection,
University of Dublin.

Nicholas Donovan 32
Courtesy of Kerry County Museum, Tralee

Evicted 40
by Lady Elizabeth Butler
Courtesy of the Irish Folklore Collection,
University of Dublin.

The Bone Saw 42
Courtesy of Kerry County Museum Tralee
Photograph by Gerald Scanlon

Jeanie Johnston Passenger Ledger 46
Courtesy of Kerry County Museum, Tralee

Emigrants at Cork 52
by Unknown Artist
Courtesy of the Irish Folklore Collection,
University of Dublin

Chart of New York harbour 1845 54
Courtesy of NOAA

Rough Weather 56–57
by Montague Dawson
Courtesy of Encore Editions, USA

Letter from America 60
by James Brennan RHA
Courtesy of the Crawford Gallery, Cork.

Original drawing for the Ship 74
by Fred M. Walker
Courtesy of the artist

Jeanie Johnston sails for America 76
by Donal Stack
Courtesy of the artist

Ship Construction Photographs 79–99
Courtesy of Peter Radclyffe – Shipwright

Lloyd's Certificate 90
Courtesy of the National Maritime Museum,
Greenwich

Jeanie Johnston Colour Scheme 97
by Fred M. Walker
Courtesy of the artist

Postage Stamp 99
Reproduced by kind permission of An Post©

Sea Fever 133
by John Masefield
Courtesy of the Society of Authors

Index

272